20 Essential Games to Study

20 Essential Games to Study

Joshua Bycer

CRC Press

Taylor & Francis Group

Boca Raton London New York

CRC Press is an imprint of the
Taylor & Francis Group, an **informa** business

CRC Press
Taylor & Francis Group
6000 Broken Sound Parkway NW, Suite 300
Boca Raton, FL 33487-2742

Printed on acid-free paper

International Standard Book Number-13: 978-1-138-34145-6 (Paperback)
978-1-138-34146-3 (Hardback)

Library of Congress Cataloging-in-Publication Data

Names: Bycer, Joshua, author.
Title: 20 essential games to study / Joshua Bycer.
Other titles: Twenty essential games to study
Description: First edition. | Boca Raton, FL : CRC Press/Taylor & Francis Group, 2019.
Identifiers: LCCN 2018029932| ISBN 9781138341456 (pbk. : acid-free paper) | ISBN 9781138341463 (hardback : acid-free paper)
Subjects: LCSH: Video games--Authorship--Case studies. | Video games--Design--Case studies.
Classification: LCC GV1469.15 .B93 2019 | DDC 794.8--dc23
LC record available at https://lccn.loc.gov/2018029932

Visit the Taylor & Francis Web site at
http://www.taylorandfrancis.com

and the CRC Press Web site at
http://www.crcpress.com

Contents

Preface

Welcome to my first book on 20 essential games to study. I have always had an interest in game design and being able to talk about the art and craft of it. Despite so many games being released, it can be very hard to break down specifically why certain games work and others don't. It's important to study why certain games have stood the test of time. The goal of this book was to pick 20 games spanning the decades and platforms that are worthy for anyone to study with an interest in game design, whether you're an experienced developer or a student.

While this list certainly has blockbusters from several major studios, I also wanted games that became cult classics due to their innovative takes on design. Great games have a sense of timelessness, and if you did not grow up playing the ones listed here, this book will expose you to some of the all-time best titles; games like *Super Metroid, X-Com UFO Defense, Devil May Cry 3*, and more. Game design is as much an art as it is a craft, and it's not something that can easily be expressed in words. Throughout this book, I'm going to go into detail about where the craftsmanship comes in and what truly distinguishes the all-time greats from everyone else.

Please let me know what you think at josh@game-wisdom.com, as I would love to continue this series with additional games or focusing on specific genres.

Author

Joshua Bycer is a game design critic who has spent more than seven years examining game design. His analytical approach has become a useful tool for developers to help improve their video games. On his website Game Wisdom (http://game-wisdom.com) and YouTube channel (http://youtube.com/c/game-wisdom), he has interviewed hundreds of game developers and members of the industry through live and recorded podcasts. The discussions he has had, and will continue to have, have helped hone his understanding of game design. He is currently one of only a handful of people who examines game design at this level of detail. Besides writing and talking about video games on a daily basis, he creates and puts on original presentations for local libraries to help educate parents and children about the games industry.

Star Control 2 (1992; PC, 3DO)

Choose Your Own Space Adventure

The late 1980s to early 1990s was a time of experimentation for the PC industry. Many of the genres that would become indicative of the platform saw their start here, along with developers trying out brand new designs.

Star Control 2 was the obvious sequel to *Star Control 1*: a game built on ship versus ship battles. For the sequel, the developers wanted to expand the scope of the game. Now taking place in the entire universe, it featured procedurally generated star systems to fill the massive game space, alongside set areas in which the story could occur.

The story involved the player returning to Earth to find it conquered by the evil race of aliens known as the Ur-Quan. With help from a space station orbiting the planet, the player had to explore the universe to find allies, rebuild their alliances, develop their flagship, and take on the Ur-Quan and their underlings.

Star Control 2 was one of several games that kept its story moving using an in-game timer. Time advanced as the player explored, and if the player was not careful, possible allies could be wiped out, and a fail state occurred if she or he took too long. To keep the story focused, specific events would appear at fixed dates to clue the player in about what they should be focusing on.

The design of the game was split among three basic **systems**, all connected via the persistence of upgrading the player's ship. Exploration was all about the player and the universe. The player was given free rein to pick a direction and start exploring, with the only limitation being the fuel supply. Each alien race had a different part of the universe as their home territory, and they would try and engage with players if they crossed into it. Outside of our solar system, the planets that you would find were procedurally built based on various conditions that affected landing.

If the player landed on a planet, the situation switched to the player controlling a simple lander to collect resources and specimens. The planet's conditions would determine the overall threat level: From thunder strikes, fire, earthquakes, and more, players had to weigh the risks of what planets to visit. Usually, the more dangerous the planet, the better the resources. Sometimes you could find a treasure planet in the universe that had the best resources, but no hazards to deal with.

The lander itself had a health status based on the number of crew using it. If the player wasn't careful, she or he could go through an entire crew or destroy the lander, requiring them to purchase a new one. The resources that you could gather would be transformed into currency to spend back at your home base. Even rarer was finding live specimens to capture, which could be traded for permanent upgrades from one of the game's alien races.

There was strategy involved in going out on expeditions in the universe. You needed to take enough fuel to allow you to head out and return, while knowing that you would be spending more every time you landed on planets. Expert players knew to be picky when it came to just dropping down on any old planet. But one planet containing the rarest resources could make the entire trip profitable.

Returning from *Star Control 1* was the combat system, which also could be played separately in Super Melee mode. Every alien ship was uniquely designed and offered different strengths and weaknesses. In Super Melee mode, each player could create a fleet out of any ship in the game to do battle with friends. The one ship that was unique to the campaign was the capital ship.

The capital ship represented the player's power and progression curve throughout playing the game. At the start, the player would have barely any fuel and only a limited crew, and the ship turned like a glacier and was just as fast. Using the resource units acquired, the ship could be upgraded so long as there was room to install modules. Play well enough, and the player would be able to increase every attribute to turn it into the greatest ship in the universe.

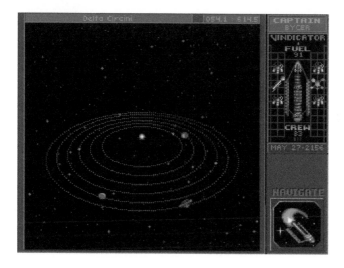

Even the mere act of increasing the turn radius and speed was enough to make the player feel powerful. If the player wanted to see the game all the way to the end, the capital ship would have to be able to take on the game's strongest alien ships.

Star Control 2 gets on this list for being one of the first examples of the "Go where you want, do what you want" style of open-world games. More important, the game managed to deliver the thrill of the space simulation genre without the learning curve or baggage that came with it.

The space simulation genre has grown in popularity thanks to both a focus on flying ships and the player having complete freedom within the game space. However, just like the **grand strategy** genre, it could be very overwhelming for new players to learn. These games tend to drop the player into the middle of everything without much guidance.

For the more complicated games, the player also must figure out how to pilot a ship. Some of the best space simulators feature a realistic physics engine to simulate what it would be like to fly a spaceship.

Even though *Star Control 2* took place in space, it did not focus at all on the sim aspect, but more on adventure. When I spoke to Paul Reiche and Fred Ford, the creators of *Star Control 2*, they both talked about being avid fans of science fiction and said that they wanted to make a game about just exploring the universe. Upgrading a ship and exploring planets were easy actions to follow, and the game's story pushed players outward into space.

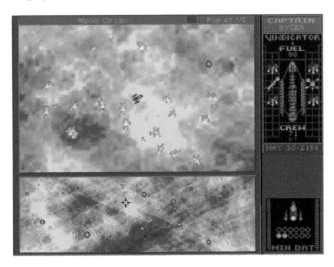

Despite the easy learning curve, *Star Control 2* was a challenge for new players. Just trying to find your way around the universe could be troublesome in and of itself. One wrong move with your lander could cost you the time that you would want to have to go out and look for more resources. As already said, the game was built on story events happening, and there was a literal end date when the Earth got destroyed.

Perhaps the best reason to check out *Star Control 2* is the fact that it's been free since the early 21st century. *Ur Quan Masters* is a fan-supported version of the game that runs on modern PCs; with the blessings of Paul and Fred.

Even though many games promise the universe to the players, *Star Control 2* is one of the few that is approachable to everyone and lets people live out their sci-fi dreams.

2

Super Metroid (1994; Super Nintendo)

The Blueprint of Metroidvania Design

When you hear the term **Metroidvania** thrown around, it usually is referring to *Castlevania: Symphony of the Night*. While that is an amazing game and one definitely worth talking about in one of these books, I want to turn to one of the games that consumers characterize as one of the best examples of the design.

Metroidvania as a term became popular following the release of *Symphony of the Night* in 1997. Assistant director Koji Igarashi drew inspiration from *The Legend of Zelda* when his team were redesigning the series for the Playstation.

Despite that, people have come to reference this design after the combination of *Castlevania* and *Metroid*.

The Metroid series, much like Nintendo's other properties, had a breakout hit in the form of *Super Metroid*. What made *Super Metroid* worthy of study was that it elevated the action genre while being one of the purest examples of Metroidvania design.

The design of *Super Metroid* was one of many popular games that moved the action genre away from just a corridor-style, linear-level design. The environment design rewarded exploration with new upgrades and paths through the game. While there was more freedom to explore, progress was gated by the upgrade system.

From bombs to missiles to the recognizable *screw attack,* of spinning through the air into enemies, they were all used to get through the various sections of the game. The system of upgrading Samus with new abilities was crucial for this entry and a major point about Metroidvania design. Simply having a character explore an environment or move a level up is not where the heart of Metroidvania design is, in my opinion. The real DNA of the genre comes in the form of the character and, by extension, the gameplay that evolves over time.

After the introduction, the player starts to find upgrades that enhance Samus in various ways. The upgrades in *Super Metroid* radically changed your movement and offensive options over the course of the game. Samus was easily controllable from the start, and she only got better over time. Super-dashing and infinite jumping were just a couple of the upgrades that players would achieve during the game.

The majority of the upgrades that could be found were those that increased the player's weapon supply and health. Many of which were hidden behind false objects, were off the beaten path, or both. While these upgrades helped the player out, the game was balanced around not needing to pick them all up.

Even though *Symphony of the Night* popularized having **RPG (Role Playing Game)** systems in Metroidvania games, that design is not a required part of Metroidvania design. The players must see growth in terms of their abilities and have the game reflect that.

Having the progression model tied to upgrades presented a world that grew just as much as Samus's moveset. Different areas of the game could be reached or maneuvered only with specific upgrades. Many areas were designed with shortcuts or alternative paths that used future upgrades. As the players acquired more upgrades, how they went through the levels changed.

Even though backtracking could be seen as a chore, being able to get around faster or take different paths helped to keep things from becoming repetitive. There was a distinct difference between playing *Super Metroid* at the beginning, middle, and end of the game. That was also reflected in the changing design of the environment. Advanced maneuvers and upgrades either led to secrets or shortcuts earlier in the game. When the player arrived at the harder areas, those once-optional tactics would be integrated into the basic routine of play.

Super Metroid avoided the trap of only designing *keys,* or upgrades that did not change the game but simply were used to get past one particular obstacle. The point about Metroidvania design was that the player's abilities should always be growing, just as the enemies and environmental obstacles should adapt to match. Lesser-quality Metroidvania games would give a player upgrades that were only meant for one specific use, and then they would never be seen again.

There was a fundamental difference in how *Super Metroid* was played from beginning to end. The major upgrades did unlock new paths, but they had secondary uses as well. One obvious example consisted of missiles and bombs used for opening doors and fighting enemies. The only key-based upgrades were in the form of Samus's suits, which allowed her to explore hot environments or move through water.

We also need to mention Samus's base abilities and how the game became popular among **speed-runners**. Despite the progression model of finding upgrades to unlock new areas, advanced maneuvers like wall jumping were available from the start, opening up the door to finding shortcuts. Expert players were able to completely bypass what had been considered required parts of the game: creating new categories to speed-run the game.

Watching speed-runners go through *Super Metroid*, there are categories designed around specifically avoiding the standard path of play or not getting standard upgrades. Playing the game at this level requires mastery of controlling Samus's movements. One of the hardest categories seen in the Metroid franchise is "low %," where the goal is to beat the game by getting as little as possible (including what were considered required upgrades).

What made this possible was that the developers limited Samus's abilities at the start, but the player was still able to make the most out of her moveset. Another knock against lesser Metroidvania games is that they purposely made the character feel unresponsive at the start, in order to create the feeling of progress. Some games start the player with slower movement, shorter jumps, or not even being able to attack at all.

The problem with this approach is that this is wasted time on the player's part, as they're unable to play the game even at the basic level. Great Metroidvania-style games make the fundamental gameplay responsive and only get better from there.

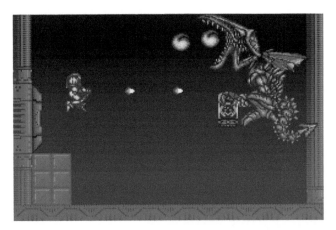

Metroidvania design has become a very popular genre among indie developers and has inspired way too many games to list here. When they work, they can be a great example of elevating two-dimensional (2D) game design. On the other hand, there is a very wide margin between the best and worst examples of the genre. It's a fascinating genre to analyze, and *Super Metroid* is one of the most amazing games to examine.

3

X-COM UFO Defense (1994; PC and Playstation 1)
Multi-System Gameplay

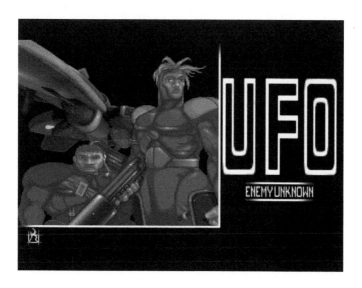

Any list exploring examples of amazing game design would not be complete without a mention of *X-COM UFO Defense*. Often regarded as one of the best games ever made, *X-COM* created its own niche within the strategy genre and was one of the most popular examples of **Multi-System Design**.

Multi-System Design refers to creating a game that features completely different game systems instead of just one. When we talk about good game design, it can

9

be viewed as all the elements coming together to create something greater than the sum of its parts. With *X-COM*, the design was really built on three separate game systems.

At the top layer, you had the *geoscape*, where the player would choose what alien attacks to respond to. The simplest of the three systems, the player's job here was to monitor the planet for UFO attacks and alien bases. The main factor of the geoscape was whether it was night or day when the player went to assault a UFO or respond to an attack, as that determined how easy it was for the troops to see. Keeping the Earth safe would determine the player's monthly funding, which at the start was required to get her or his base up and running.

If the player did not respond to alien attacks in time, the different countries would become unhappy with him or her, to the point of pulling out of the organization and siding with the aliens. Eventually, the player would have to assault alien bases that were discovered at the geoscape layer.

One layer down was *managing the base and economy*. Bases were completely customizable by the player, and she or he could build multiple ones so long as there were the funds for it. Bases could research new technology that then could be manufactured and used, or sold for money. If the players did their job right, they would be able to earn all the money they would need via making items and selling them to the black market. The bases also operated as launching platforms for sending out troops and attacking UFOs. The layout of the base was taken into account if the aliens invaded, and they could destroy the base if the player didn't defend it.

The final layer was the tactical strategy of *commanding troops in the field*. The original *X-COM* was built on a simulation defined by **RPG** rules, with survival never guaranteed. The units, or "squaddies," as they were known as, were very weak at the start. The player only had access to basic rifles and no armor at the beginning; it was common to lose several units on the very first mission.

The tactical layer was advanced for its time thanks to its RPG foundation. There were numerous stats related to your weapons and squaddies. Attributes like bravery, reaction time, and accuracy came to define each member of your squad. Weapons had different firing modes that each cost a number of time units (Tus) to use. TUs dictated how much each squaddie could do in a single turn, and having a lot of them was prized by players.

Every time you hire a new squaddie, the values of its attributes were randomly assigned. Expert players did their best to cultivate the best starting rookies into full-fledged alien hunters. Even if you did get unlucky, squaddies who would survive to get promotions also would receive increases to their attributes.

The genius of *X-COM* was how the systems interacted and fed off of each other. Managing the geoscape gave the player an idea of where alien threats were coming from and where to build bases. The bases would provide enhancements and upgrades for the other two layers. Items and squaddies would be used during the tactical layer, and the player could upgrade ships for better combat at the geoscape layer. How well someone played during the tactical battles would net items that could be sold or researched back at the base to unlock new gear and upgrades. Through upgrades, the troops would go from wearing basic uniforms and using assault rifles to using alien laser weapons with flight suits and psychic commandos as backup.

X-COM's Multi-System Design created a progression curve that went through all three game systems. The reason why *X-COM* would be considered multi-system was because each system was its own separate entity, with different elements, control, and **UI**. The connection between the systems was in the form of progression, which meant that the player was moving forward in one way or another.

Having a bad battle where the player lost all the squaddies could be made up by the fact that the player got what he or she needed to create new weapons. *X-COM* was also one of the first examples of a game featuring a nonlinear campaign. Every successful game ended with a trip to Mars to fight the alien leader, but players were free to decide when to start the final mission.

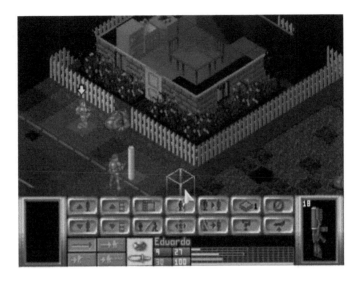

One understated aspect of *X-COM*'s design was how it became the foundation for player-made storytelling. There have been multiple AARs (**After Action Reports**) written by fans who transformed a tactical battle into an epic drama unfolding on the battlefield. Even though the player couldn't personalize the characters as in later entries, that didn't stop people from naming their squaddies after friends, family, or people they didn't like.

X-COM's difficulty would grow over the course of playing the game, with new and harder aliens introduced over time, which became synonymous with the series. These aliens ranged from the classic sectoids, or "Greys," to the destructive power of chrysalids, who could turn civilians and friends alike into zombies. Due to the procedural design of the tactical maps, the player had to prepare for anything. Eventually, one of two things would happen: The player had a fully upgraded squad ready to take on the final mission or would be overwhelmed by the alien attacks.

X-COM's design to this day is not something that can be easily replicated. The granularity of detail when it came to the RPG systems was overwhelming to new players. There were numerous weapons, grenades, specialty items, and other features to give to squaddies. While the player could use up everyone's TUs, a far more important strategy was conserving it for what was known as a *reaction fire*, where characters could attack the other team during their turn.

The use of reaction fire became one of the tensest moments when playing *X-COM*, as assaulting an UFO would lead to the player entering a room of reaction-ready aliens, all trained on their squaddies.

Understanding the tactical use of TUs, reaction fire, and how they related to combat was vital. Gaining or losing squaddies with high-enough stats created powerful swings in balance. A full squad of promoted squaddies in the best gear could easily wreck anything that the game could throw at the player. Conversely, the player's chance of surviving the final mission without them was low. This was one of those games that were hard to learn, but easy to break once players knew what they were doing.

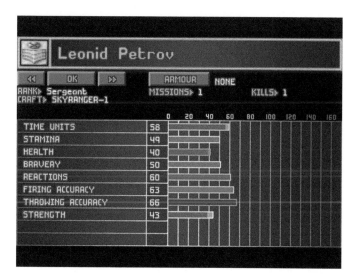

Even at that point, the random nature of *X-COM*'s systems still led to surprising situations—from missing what was supposed to be a guaranteed shot to a squaddie somehow surviving hit after hit. Nothing in *X-COM* was 100 percent guaranteed, and players quickly learned that harsh lesson.

When Firaxis Games decided to attempt its own reboot of the franchise, it created new underlining systems instead of trying to create a direct sequel to the original. In return, *XCOM: Enemy Unknown* (and *XCOM2*) featured more board game design compared to *X-COM*'s RPG design. Regardless, *XCOM* is also worthy of being an entry in this series that we may come back to at some point.

Multi-System game design may not work for every designer, but it's another way of building a game to create something greater than the sum of its parts. The fact that we can still talk about *X-COM* more 20 years after its invention is a testament to its original design.

4

The Logical Journey of the Zoombinis (1996; PC)
A Rewarding Experience

© 2015 TERC - Reproduced with permission.

Edutainment was a popular buzzword during the 1990s as video game culture grew. The dream of using video games to provide educational value has been chased by many developers over the years. Trying to achieve the balance between having engaging gameplay and educating users is not easy. You could end up either with something that has too little educational value for it to work or not enough gameplay to keep someone's attention.

Edutainment also faced the challenge in public schools of teaching to what was known as the "common core." The common core, first created in 2009, was a set of state-defined standards for teaching K–12 students in terms of

English and mathematics. Not only that, but video games can be harder to use to test someone's accumulated knowledge compared to traditional lessons and testing.

The 1990s saw a big push by software companies to get into the education market and school systems; with companies like Broderbund and The Learning Company being two of the bigger ones. We saw games designed to teach history, math, electricity, and many more subjects. For my money, the best and arguably most successful edutainment game was *The Logical Journey of the Zoombinis*.

Long before gamers would fall in love with the *Professor Layton* series and the growth of the casual puzzle market, *The Logical Journey of the Zoombinis* (or just *Zoombinis* for the rest of this entry) was a game designed to teach children critical thinking skills.

The plot had the player relocating the Zoombini population from their island home that was taken over by another race of creatures. The only thing standing in the way of this worthy goal was a series of **minigames**, each built as its own kind of puzzle.

Each of the minigames presented in *Zoombinis* was built around a different kind of puzzle-solving tactic, including deductive reasoning, hypothesis testing, and so on. The objective was to figure out how to get your group of Zoombinis past the challenge and get a full group of 16 to their new home. You could customize each Zoombini in terms of its appearance, which would show up as a factor in several minigames.

Several puzzles would base their solutions on a specific feature of the Zoombini. The very first puzzle required the player to figure out what specific part would be blocked by crossing set bridges.

Zoombinis bucked the trend of other edutainment titles at the time—it was about engaging the player with gameplay instead of schoolwork. The bright graphics and crazy situations helped to mask the fact that children were learning critical thinking skills. Other edutainment titles at the time focused on the learning side first, with gameplay second or even third on the list. In these cases, the gameplay of the title was simply a means to get to the next math problem or history lesson, with a famous example being the game *Mario Is Missing*. Any actual gameplay was kept on the basic side to prevent distraction from the educational aspects.

What helped *Zoombinis* to gain its cult following and a place on this list was how the designers looked to the future to get children to keep playing. Long before anyone heard of **achievements** in video games, *Zoombinis* featured an effective reward system.

The player could beat the game by simply getting small groups of Zoombinis to Zoombiniville over however many hours of play, but the most efficient way was getting a complete group there. Every time the player succeeded, the game would reward him or her with a new building.

The minigames that the player encountered on that path would be bumped up in difficulty. The puzzles themselves would remain the same in terms of the goal, but more variables would be introduced to raise the challenge level. This could include adding in factors or reducing the number of times that the player could mess up without penalty. Due to the requirement of getting a full group, kids were not exposed to challenges they weren't ready for. In essence, they would let the game know by earning the achievements.

The use of camps on the map allowed the player to recover lost Zoombinis sometimes and complete an unfinished group. Every design decision was meant to keep children invested in learning and be rewarded for it.

Zoombiniville itself is the perfect example of what I call **Trophy Room Design**, or having an in-game representation of player achievements. It was the perfect motivation to show players that they're improving and recognize their achievements. A player could look at all the buildings earned (with plaques commemorating the dates of the achievements), and even print out certificates.

Despite being aimed at children and the edutainment market, *Zoombinis* showed an elegant design that appealed to all fans of the puzzle genre. The reward system obviously worked, as achievements have become almost standard across the entire game industry today. Integrating the puzzle design into both the **gamespace** and the difficulty system allowed people to play at their own pace; they never felt rushed to play through.

Typical adventure and puzzle games present their challenges as locked doors: Players cannot move on until they solve a puzzle to unlock each door. In *Zoombinis*, every puzzle had a limit based on the number of Zoombinis in your group and the number of turns. It was not possible for a player to become completely stuck at a puzzle, as eventually the game will just move the person along with whatever Zoombinis were saved.

Good achievement design is not about giving out participation trophies, but about rewarding accomplishment with positive feedback. If players wanted to get all the buildings unlocked in Zoombiniville, they had to work for it, but no matter how good or poor they were at the game, they eventually got to the ending.

Long before the puzzle genre would blow up in the casual space, *Zoombinis* was creating a generation of gamers who grew up playing critical thinking puzzles. *Zoombinis* showed a surprising amount of forward thinking in terms of game design, and it deserves to be studied by designers regardless of the age group they're aiming to please.

5

Goldeneye 64 (1997; Nintendo 64)

Bringing the FPS to the Consoles

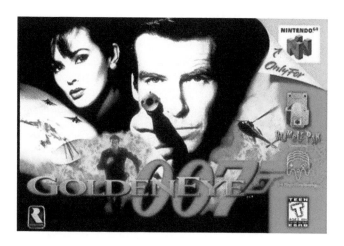

Since its inception, the First Person Shooter, or FPS, genre has been one of the dividing points between console and PC gamers. Due to the control system of the keyboard (and eventually the mouse as well), FPS were considered to be playable only on PCs. Any FPS that was ported to consoles was considered lesser and not as well designed as their PC counterparts. While console-exclusive FPS were released during the 1990s, the lack of mouse look greatly limited the player's control.

Mouse look was, and still is, an essential element of why the PC has been the superior platform for FPS games. The mouse combined aiming and shooting into one peripheral and freed the other hand for basic motions. By tying aiming and camera control directly to the mouse movement, it allows for a 1:1 aiming control for instant positioning. As a secondary benefit, it allowed designers more freedom in level design and enemy placements, taking into account how easy it was to adjust for elevation.

To rub even more salt in the wound, consoles were behind the PC in terms of providing a multiplayer architecture that would allow people to play against each other. Even with dial-up modems, gamers were playing games on their computers long before consoles came with a built-in modem. *Goldeneye* (otherwise known as *Goldeneye 64*) was the first game to give console fans a completely original FPS interface, but it also came the closest to providing a multiplayer experience like the PC.

Developed by Rare, *Goldeneye* had a lot to prove out of the gate, as it was not only a console FPS, but a game based on a licensed property—in this case being the movie by the same name. Many of the games that were considered the worst of their time were built on licensed properties because often, the gameplay had little relation to the movie. *Goldeneye*'s story followed the plot of the movie, with players controlling 007 through the iconic set pieces.

For the time, *Goldeneye* was one of the most advanced shooter games in terms of playability. While a full mouse look was not possible due to the controller, players could free-aim shots and strafe to avoid gunfire. Besides featuring a variety of guns, *Goldeneye* was one of the first FPS games to give additional tools to the player beyond those for shooting. Laser watches, remote mines, and other weapons were available to help the player complete the game's many objectives.

The level design of *Goldeneye* was impressive thanks to the variety of environments and missions. While there were plenty of action levels, players also had to deal with stealth sections. If the player was detected, an alarm would sound, triggering infinite spawns of enemies. Some levels had basic puzzles for the player to solve in order to complete objectives.

One of the best parts of the campaign was how Rare handled difficulties. The difficulty settings of *Goldeneye* not only raised the damage enemies did but added new objectives. For new players, the easier settings allowed them to rush through the levels with impunity. On the higher settings, the objectives would take players to additional areas of the map while also having them deal with increased aggression from the enemies. This system was also seen in Rare's spiritual follow-up, *Perfect Dark*.

While the campaign was one of the best of its time, the real reason that people remember *Goldeneye* to this day is that Rare was delivering the first great FPS multiplayer experience off the PC. *Goldeneye* allowed up to four players at a time to play in a variety of modes using all the weapons from the main game. The Nintendo 64 was the first home console to really show off the potential of multiplayer games, and *Goldeneye* was one of the top experiences. While online play wasn't possible at this time, *Goldeneye* was an amazing party game.

The game came with different modes to play with, and included modifiers like "one-shot kill" to allow players to create their own situations. The idea of creating custom game modes via modifiers would be translated later into *Perfect Dark* and to other console shooters throughout the years.

No one knew this at the time, but *Goldeneye 64* laid the groundwork for console multiplayer experiences; ranging from the likes of *Halo* to *Call of Duty*, and many more. In today's market, it's now unheard of to release a shooter game on consoles without multiplayer capability. Most developers will release separate servers for the console and PC audiences in order to prevent the PC side from having an inherent control advantage with the keyboard and mouse.

Even though multiplayer and online design has evolved considerably since the days of *Goldeneye*, it still has important lessons for game designers today. With enough ingenuity, it is possible to take genres that people consider to be platform locked and bring them to new platforms, and potentially new fans.

This past decade has seen console and PC developers embracing each other's side, with the consumer winning by getting access to more titles. The fact that we're seeing Japanese publishers like Bandai Namco do same-day release for their console and PC titles is proof of this.

You still have to recognize the quirks or limitations of moving from console, PC, or mobile, and redesign your game accordingly. You cannot take a genre and just port it 1:1 and expect it to do well. You'll need to work to accommodate the new platform and any quality-of-life features unique to it.

With *Goldeneye*, the developers knew that the Nintendo 64 control pad could not emulate the same fidelity that a keyboard and mouse affords. Instead of trying to chase that perfection, they designed around it by making a game suitable to the platform. This also meant adjusting the enemy **AI** (Artificial Iintelligence) and level structure for the slower motions of the gamepad.

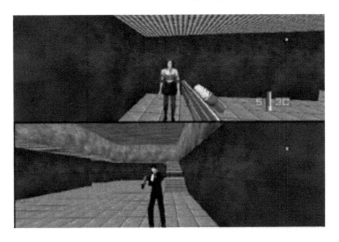

Regardless of its changes and accommodations, *Goldeneye* worked as a game from the FPS genre. You could see a similar philosophy in the Nintendo hit *Pikmin* that streamlined real-time strategy commands for the Nintendo GameCube market. Being able to understand your limitations is an important step in refining your game concept.

Goldeneye, along with titles like *Turok*, proved that original FPS could work on the console side with the right design. Even though online play wasn't yet in the cards, the multiplayer architecture was starting to develop on the console. If it can work, don't be afraid to bring a different kind of genre to a new platform; you never know what the potential is for a brand new group of fans to fall in love with it.

Metal Gear Solid
(1998; Playstation 1)
Tactical Espionage Gameplay

Merging designs to create new genres has become a popular pastime over the last decade. It has led to popular series like *Borderlands, Call of Duty,* and *Dark Souls,* to name a few. However, two of the most polarizing genres would be action and stealth. One rewards running around and fighting, while the other is all about patience and being methodical.

Many game designers have tried to get them to fit together, but their efforts have often led to one genre overpowering the other. Sometimes the player is punished too much for breaking stealth, or it's just easier and safer to kill every enemy.

The *Metal Gear* series was one of the first to combine action and stealth design, and it was further iterated on with the *Solid* series. Instead of presenting a game that was either action or stealth, *Metal Gear Solid* (and its sequels) integrated the two together.

Each game was about the player taking on the role of Snake, the ultimate solider and infiltrator. He was skilled in using a variety of weapons, hand-to-hand combat, and stealth to avoid detection. The game ultimately rewarded the player for being sneaky but did not hinder their ability to fight if the need arose. Snake was always given multiple types of guns, bombs, traps, and other tools to use at the player's will. Despite that, many players would forgo them in favor of the stealth system.

Many stealth games are built on a "pass-or-fail" nature that once the player was discovered, she or he would lose. This could be due to the game just ending or the player having no way to reenter stealth. We see the latter in many action games that implement stealth sections, where once the player was spotted, every enemy on the map was alerted. One of the most infamous designs during the 1990s and early 2000s created action games that introduced forced stealth sections for which the rest of the design was not built. This included clunky controls, inconsistent detection systems, basic enemy AI, and more.

By using the variety of weapons at their disposal in *Metal Gear Solid*, it was possible for players to fight their way out of bad situations and sometimes evade their pursuers to reinitialize stealth. Even with the focus on stealth, the action never felt limited or downplayed. This was especially true for the series's focus on amazing and memorable boss fights.

You like Castlevania, don't you?

The bosses in the *Metal Gear Solid* series ran the gambit of stealth, action, or a combination of both. No two bosses were ever designed the same, and each one required the player to use of all the available options to defeat it. *Metal Gear Solid* had an amazing cast of enemies for Snake to take on, the most famous being Psycho Mantis, who forced the player to switch the controller port on the system to "confuse him."

This was one of only a few games in the grand scheme of the industry where boss fights were always welcomed, just to see what new crazy design the team had in mind for the player. Every boss had its own unique abilities and rules for fighting it. One of the more clever forms of challenge started in

Metal Gear Solid 2: Sons of Liberty, which introduced the added optional goal of fighting every boss without using lethal weapons.

The *Metal Gear Solid* series deserves praise for the variety of tools that the player could use. With each game in the series, the player's toolset and options grew to create an almost sandbox atmosphere—affording the player a variety of ways to solve the game's challenges. Fans know just how crazy the number of tactics you could employ in the series. From holding enemies up for items and intel to the infamous cardboard box, and literally hiding in plain sight—the series gave the player freedom to explore and figure out how to play. A good example was from *Metal Gear Solid 3,* which literally allowed the player to beat a fight by moving the system clock ahead a few weeks.

Having this freedom goes back to how *Metal Gear Solid* as a franchise really became its own genre in the eyes of players. To this day, it's still one of only a few series to understand the different pulls of stealth and action—hence the moniker "Tactical Espionage Action."

As the player, you could feel just as powerful running around shooting up enemies as sneaking through a military base undetected. Even though the game graded and ranked players on how well they stayed hidden throughout the game, there were always multiple ways of getting through a tough spot.

During this era, video games and storytelling were still considered only as a niche market for kids, but series creator and designer Hideo Kojima had a different idea. *Metal Gear Solid* was one of the first games to incorporate cinematography to create the feel of watching a movie. Cut scenes, both small and very large, were fully voiced, which helped to propel voice actors like David Hayter to video game stardom.

While other series were using stories like "save the princess," the *Metal Gear* series told a complex (and arguably convoluted) story about secret societies, war, genetics, and much more, with these themes growing over the course of the main series. Even being the first game in the series, *Metal Gear Solid*'s story had all manners of twists and turns, along with callbacks to the original games also made by Kojima.

When designing your game, don't take whatever genre you're focusing on as law when it comes to **mechanics**. You can always do more in the action genre than just fighting everything, just as stealth can mean more than just hiding in the shadows. *Metal Gear Solid* presents proof that you can think outside the (cardboard) box to create something entirely unique.

No matter how far the action and stealth genres will evolve, the *Metal Gear Solid* franchise stands on its own without compromising either aspect. The series, with all its quirks, is one of a kind and helped propel Kojima to superstar status among developers. Stealth and action game design don't have to be mutually exclusive, and *Metal Gear Solid* is a happy marriage between the two.

7

Diablo II (2000; PC)
The Art of Loot

The action role-playing game (**ARPG**) genre comes in many forms, but there is only one *Diablo*. Developed by Blizzard Entertainment, we could easily focus on any of the three main games in the series regarding its impact and legacy.

The reason why I chose *Diablo II* for this book was how this game fully cemented the allure and chasing of loot. *Loot* is the common term for any item that can be found in an RPG, and the *Diablo* series has built a franchise on it.

Loot was procedurally generated as the players fought enemies in the field. They never knew what they were going to find (with the exception of buying items at the shops). The beauty of the loot system was how it became the driving force of playing *Diablo II: Lord of Destruction*, and by extension ARPG design. Loot was broken down by class, type, rarity, and stats or modifiers. The higher the rarity, the better the gear. It wasn't just about the stats, as better gear would change the look of your character, with higher qualities having better detail.

Each piece of gear above normal quality that would drop in *Diablo II* was procedurally generated to be different. The modifiers that could appear ranged from simply increasing stats to directly affecting specific class skills.

Loot generation was handled by a **loot table**, a system designed to generate gear procedurally based on a number of set values defined by the game developer and then randomly chosen by the game engine. This system is required in any game where you want the player to always be finding original gear.

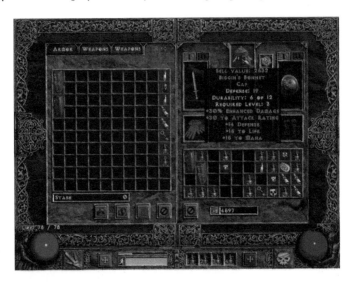

Getting it to work is no easy task. Not only do you need to make sure that the game is generating gear correctly, but it also needs to scale properly to the player's current challenge. That last point was a major issue and the reason why people hated the original release of *Diablo III*.

The problem was that the possible scaling in terms of power was so wide that there came a point where the chance of finding upgrades became too small. At the highest difficulty of the launch version of *Diablo III*, the player either blew away the enemies by getting lucky (or using the auction house) or got beaten into dust by the overtuned enemies.

This is why many games feature the ability to scale loot tables based on the player's or enemy's level. By constantly scaling the loot table values higher, it gives the player the chance of finding something better and keeping pace with the enemies' power curve.

The number of varying factors in terms of loot generation is why it can be hard to know how to balance the game. From a design point of view, you can have a rough idea of what the player's power level will be based on the available loot tables, but it is never exact. Just as you can have players who found all the best gear and are destroying the game, you will have those who are just barely getting by.

Modern game designers try to abstract the player's power via a gear-rating system. The system grades the players based on the gear they're wearing to give a rough estimate of how strong they are at the moment. While not perfect, it does provide a ballpark figure in terms of balancing the enemy's attributes.

Due to the variance of loot, ARPG design always features a second form of progressing. The other half of *Diablo II*'s progression model was leveling up your character. Killing enemies and completing quests would give players experience points. After leveling up, they could apply points to their characters' base stats and unlock new abilities on their skill trees. Each class in the game had three unique skill trees to build players' characters.

A player could either spread the points around to make a jack-of-all-trades character or make a very specific build. With each class being completely different from one another, there were many different ways to play the game. Players' skills could be further improved by getting the right modifiers on their gear.

What made *Diablo II* worthy of being studied was how far the rabbit hole went in terms of the power curve. The highest tiers in the game belonged to Set and Unique items. Set items were a group of items that belonged together, with the more pieces in a set collected added to their power, while Unique items had some of the highest stats in the game and had their own styles to differentiate them.

Diablo II also had other options in the form of rune words, tablets that could be inserted into gear. If the player inserted the right order and combination of runes into an item, it would be transformed into a unique piece of gear.

Despite all the possible variances of modifiers and gears that could be generated, it was still easy as a player to see what worked for a particular class. The expansion to *Diablo II* added class-specific items to diversify the loot pool further. While players could use generic gear, class-specific gear typically had bonuses that were directly related to playing the specified class.

The loot design of *Diablo II* worked better than with *Diablo III*, even after a 1.04 patch was added to improve the game. *Diablo III*'s loot design had a literal end point in terms of pure progression. After a player got the set that she or he wanted for the class in question, there were no other forms of meaningful progression at the end game. Players couldn't create custom gear or upgrade their gear beyond having ancient set items (the highest class of items added after the expansion). Coupled with the lower-level cap, this led to a very plain end game.

The stat variance problem at *Diablo III*'s launch has now been reversed. The game is now rigidly defined by the loot tables tied to the player's level. Once a player hits the cap, any further progression is locked to set items that have the highest possible stat values.

Even though there were set items in *Diablo II*, there was more room for variation and customization in terms of your build. The controversial move from skill trees to builds may have made *Diablo III* more streamlined, but it came at the cost of customization. Tying back into the set design, there were only a handful of ways of playing *Diablo III*'s end game via set-related bonuses. To their credit, Blizzard did release additional sets for their seasons, but without new skills or class growth, you were still picking from the same hard-coded choices.

In *Diablo II*, a player was free to fully customize a character in terms of skills. In return, it allowed far more utility of gear at the end game compared to *Diablo III* and made it less likely for players to hit the power wall.

As a player, you never knew just when that next powerful upgrade would drop, and that motivated people to keep pushing on through the game. The only set notion in terms of loot generation was that the further the player got into the game, the stronger the gear that would appear. The cycle of "Kill Enemies, Gather Loot, Grow Stronger" pushed players to the higher difficulty levels. And when a game gets that cycle right, fans will have a title that keeps bringing them back for more and more.

Half-Life 2 (2004; PC and Multiple Platforms)

Sectional Design

The *Half-Life* series is one of the most famous in terms of the game industry. Even though many people will only recognize its success as part of Valve's rise with the introduction of Steam, there is more to examine in terms of its design.

A typical style of game design is that once the design or structure of the game has been set, that's how it remains for the entirety of the experience. The closest analog would be the categorizing of movies and shows based on specific genres. *Half-Life* and *Half-Life 2* were not structured like other games. Valve built the series as a collection of sections, as opposed to just one design.

This kind of **Sectional Design** kept the game from repeating content and gameplay, while continuing to challenge the player with new situations. Sections such as surviving the headcrab-infested town of Ravenholm, riding a hovercraft, and driving through the desert changed how someone would play *Half-Life 2* beyond just FPS gameplay. The game never took the player completely out of the **core gameplay loop**; it simply added or subtracted elements based on where they were at any given time.

To be fair to other game designs, we have seen plenty of action games throw in a unique section to mix up the gameplay, but it often felt forced and never on the same level as the rest of the content. In *Half-Life 2*, each section was given just as much care and polish as the rest, while standing out with its own situations. The sections never felt as though the player was just going through the motions to get back to the action; rather, they were based on the situation and story at hand.

The beginning of the game was chase-focused, as the player was trying to get out of City 17. The story was that the series' hero, Gordon Freeman, has returned to a world occupied by an alien race known as the Combine. At the start, the player was introduced to basic combat and the starting enemy types while being chased around. Things start to slow down once the player evaded capture by the Combine soldiers, and then new enemies and situations were introduced.

The idea behind Sectional Design is to create designs that exist within their own microlayer while still representing the game as a whole. The split focus also made the world of *Half-Life 2* feel greater than the sum of its parts. One of the hovercraft sections combined FPS combat, exploration, vehicular driving, and puzzle-solving into a single experience. Even though the hovercraft itself was used in several other sections, it never felt like Valve was just reusing the same gameplay repeatedly.

Once a section was finished, that exact gameplay was not repeated, despite the obvious temptation to use it to pad out the game. Even the shooting felt different based on the environment and enemies that the player was facing. Fighting the slow-moving enemies of Ravenholm was a brief reprieve from the armies of the

Combine. Far too many action games will repeat gameplay content (the video game equivalent of the "rule of threes") to drag things out. In *Half Life 2,* the game kept on adding in new elements until the very end.

In the second-to-last major section of *Half-Life 2,* the player used light squad management of resistance members before the final battle into the Citadel. This kind of gameplay was used only in that one section, and for a limited time, before throwing the player into the finale.

Half Life 2 managed to strike that happy medium between keeping the gameplay from getting out of hand with too many choices, or being too constricting with just repeating the same gameplay loop from beginning to end. Every section in the game was always built on the same basic mechanics that players always had access to. They could move, shoot, jump, and pick up objects to throw. Outside the vehicle sections, the player's core actions were always available; it was just that the actual use differed.

No matter what part of the game the player was in, it still felt great to play. The *Half Life* series was about slower-paced combat compared to its peers like *Unreal* or *Doom.* Players were free to run and gun, but they had to play it smart and engage with enemies when the time was right.

Half Life 2 also introduced gamers to the gravity gun, which would become one of the most iconic weapons in a FPS. The gravity gun allowed them to pick up almost anything that wasn't nailed down so it could be used as a weapon or shield. Combine that with the game's physics engine, and players were launching paint cans, bricks, saw blades, and more at the various enemies. One of the most memorable parts of the game was the very last section, when at long last the gravity gun was able to grab enemies directly to kill them.

Lesser games that try to mix genres or designs tend to make players feel like they have to finish their vegetables before getting back to the main course. You had action games, which would throw in a very loose driving segment, or stealth games, which had forced combat. The reason why this didn't work was that the core gameplay loop was not meant to accommodate the various genres. These additional sections either tried to tack on new mechanics or try and fit the existing ones into them.

Even the *Grand Theft Auto* series, which is considered one of the best at combining genres, sometimes has a tough time balancing shooting, driving, and hand-to-hand combat, all with the same core gameplay loop and UI. Those reasons alone were why mixing genres were looked at negatively by gamers, and many great games often had that one bad level in them.

Half Life 2's core gameplay loop was flexible to allow for the different sections. At the same time, the designers would focus on specific parts of the loop for each section. Several areas would challenge the player with platforming without any direct threat, just as the player would get caught in firefights in constricted areas.

Half-Life 2 was also a major example of environmental storytelling in a video game. So much about what happened to the world and the state of things could be seen by looking around as the player. Instead of stopping the flow for exposition, players could wander around and put the pieces together themselves.

From the sterile environment of City 17 to the utter devastation of Ravenholm, they painted a picture of a dying, conquered world. The game did not take complete control away from the player to focus on a cutscene. Most moments of exposition still allowed the player to walk around and remain in control. Watching and listening to the developer's commentary, I was amazed to see the process that went on at Valve to guide players through the game without them knowing it.

Sectional Design is not thinking about your game as just another FPS or just another platformer, but defining distinct areas of gameplay that become greater than the sum of their parts.

9

Katamari Damacy (2004; Playstation 2)
Simplistic Beauty

Figuring out what is good and bad game design is a topic worthy of its own book. For a lot of gamers, there is this opinion that an easy game cannot be an amazing game, but one of the hallmarks of great game design is creating something that is both simple and engaging.

Katamari Damacy was born out of a school project from lead designer Keita Takahashi to create something easily enjoyed by anyone. The gameplay consisted of the player rolling around a giant ball, or katamari, in a variety of environments. Because the game is physics-based, the ball's velocity changes depending on what objects would get stuck to it. The level would end when the player reached a certain size or rolled up specific objects depending on the level.

Of the games featured in this book, *Katamari Damacy* is definitely the simplest in terms of design, but it was the complete package that helped transcended the game into pop culture. The visual design was a surreal fantasy of a prince rolling a ball around while exploring a cartoon take on real life. You could roll up everything—trash, people, weather events, and more. The aesthetics of the game have aged well, thanks to a focus of surrealism versus detail.

As the game went on, the scale of the environment grew to match the size of the katamari. One level had the players start at street level, and by the end, they were literally rolling up continents. This was further expanded with the cutscenes and general story. The King of all Cosmos, after a destructive night, broke all the stars in the sky. To repair the damage, he forced his son to collect enough stuff with the katamaris to create new stars.

Any discussion of *Katamari Damacy*'s appeal cannot ignore the soundtrack. Featuring an entirely original set of songs, the music works with the visuals to tie everything together. The soundtrack of *Katamari Damacy* is easily one of my all-time favorites, thanks to the variety of genres.

Katamari Damacy was one of those games that were just a joy to play. The control scheme was another example of the game's simple genius. The player used both analog sticks to simulate pushing the katamari around, and alternating really fast would let the player dash around. Turning the katamari was simulated by pressing only one of the sticks as an analog of just pushing half of it. The intuitiveness of the controls adhered to Keita's vision of a game that anyone could play.

The affordance of simulating pushing via the analog sticks meant that it was easy to relate what you were doing on the gamepad in relation to what was happening on screen. Most video games have to abstract the player's commands to the in-game action, which can make it harder for new players to learn. With *Katamari Damacy*, it didn't take long for anyone to start rolling, running, and picking everything up.

Instead of trying to create a progression curve that made the game more complex over time, the developers simply increased the scope of the game space and the amount of time that the player would spend on each level. The first level had a timer of three minutes, compared to the final level, at twenty-five minutes.

What made *Katamari Damacy* an important game to look at was how the series avoided the stigma of other simplistic titles. From a gameplay point of view, even though *Katamari Damacy* was simple to play, it offered ways of pushing the player. Instead of some levels just ending when the player reached the requested size, you could keep on playing to set a new record for that level.

Levels that required the player to collect one specific item forced her or him to try and control the katamari to pick up the best version of the item. It may sound easy, but given the chaotic nature of controlling the katamari to begin with, these levels became the hardest for players to master.

Many games aimed at the casual scene target only casual players, which is why they are often looked down upon by core gamers. *Katamari Damacy* kept track of each player's score and pushed everyone to do better—Replaying levels to create bigger and more elaborate stars.

As an added bonus, hidden rewards in the form of new clothing for the prince (and new characters, in later games) were spread out in gift boxes throughout the levels. For people interested in **speed-running**, the game offered a lot in terms of finding the best and fastest way to the goal. Having the katamari's physics affected by what was attached to it created an entirely new set of challenges for speed-running the game.

Due to how the physics of the katamari changed depending on what was attached, it required players to not only know the best path through the level, but constantly adjust their control based on the velocity. Attaching oddly shaped objects like cars or mountains would prevent the katamari from rolling smoothly. Conversely, these objects would push the katamari higher up in the air and could help when it came to navigating low objects.

But again, the beauty of the design was that the complexity of movement was not built into the control of the game. It was easy to see how the different objects stuck to the katamari would change how it moved. Even the best players at the game couldn't roll the katamari perfectly in terms of item placement. The series was always about managing the controlled chaos of how weird moving the katamari would become. No matter how the player grew the katamari, it was still possible to beat any level at the basic requirements.

Everything together made *Katamari Damacy* greater than the sum of its parts. A common pitfall of games with streamlined gameplay is that the developer just stops once it comes up with the core gameplay loop and doesn't try to build on it. In return, the game quickly becomes repetitive to play. Here, the sheer spectacle of everything happening holds the player's attention, with small changes via the level design that prevent the game from feeling repetitive. *Katamari Damacy* and its sequels will never be labeled as complex games, but there's enough here for casual and core players to enjoy.

10

Devil May Cry 3 (2005; Playstation 2)

Bringing Style to the Action Genre

The action genre has been a favorite of mine since its inception. The focus on player skill with the over-the-top nature of combat has been an effective formula. A good action game is like designing a supercar or a high-quality watch: It's all about precision and perfection. The player must be in control of the character at all times, while still making combat dynamic and interesting for repeated plays.

That last part is a problem that I have with modern action games that tend to devolve into the same hit string repeated over how many hours of play. When I think about my top action games, the one that nails the dynamic and improvisation of fighting that I'm looking for is *Devil May Cry 3 (DMC 3)*.

After the failure of *Devil May Cry 2 (DMC 2)*, Capcom had to go back to the drawing board with *DMC 3*. While a prequel, the game was the most forward thinking in terms of design and gameplay. What earns the game a spot on this list is the combat system.

In general, action games tend to feature two extremes in terms of combat. There are plenty that have basic button combos and repeating the same actions. The other kind has the feel of a more fighting game, with elaborate combos and different attack styles. The dividing point comes down to one simple question: Was the game designed around 1 v 1 or 1 v many fights?

One-on-one combat allows higher depth, with attacks designed to be quick to allow fast reactions. There is usually an ebb and flow to the combat, with positioning being a major part of defense and offense. Most of the time, 1 v 1 combat is slower than group battles, as the enemies are usually more advanced in their patterns and attacks.

Group-focused combat makes use of slower but wider combos meant to attack groups of enemies. For group-based games, the enemies are more about mobbing the player than individually providing a challenge. These games typically are faster-paced than 1 v 1 games, due to the chaotic nature of fighting groups. One drawback was that combat of this kind tends to be loose, and it could be hard to fight and pick out single targets.

Due to the slower attacks, you could end up with the player performing a combat action and having the enemies dodge out of the way, but she or he was still stuck in the combo string.

DMC 3 was focused on 1 v 1, and the other enemies just happen to get caught in the crossfire. Each weapon that Dante could use had its own move-list associated to it. Some examples would be the rapid nature of the Cerberus nunchucks or the charge-focused Beowulf gauntlets. While this did increase the learning curve for playing the game, it allowed players to essentially craft their own combos by switching weapons during an attack.

To add further complexity to the gameplay, *DMC 3* was the first game in the series to use styles for Dante. Various styles were designed to allow a player to focus on a specific strategy during play. The trickster improved Dante's agility and made it easier to dodge attacks, while the sword master improved the functionality of his melee attacks.

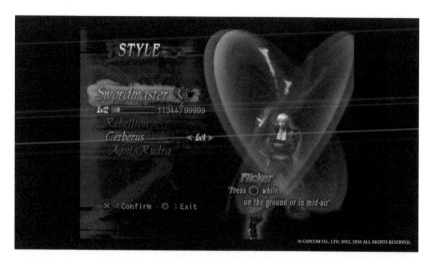

To this day, *DMC 3* is still one of the most complicated action games, thanks to the options mentioned. While each game in the series has ranked players, this is the only time where, for me, getting the coveted SSS rank felt like a real accomplishment. The player's grade was based on not getting hit, continuing to put pressure on the enemy, and most important, not repeating the same combo string.

Expert players who wanted to show off had to balance attacking the enemies and avoiding their attacks, throwing in a taunt here and there, and making sure to keep mixing up the attacks between their two equipped weapons. This was truly a game based on players earning style points.

The basic enemies of an action game are always treated as appetizers to the boss fights, and *DMC 3* was no exception. While not as showy as games like *God of War*, the bosses of *DMC 3* was a popular example of the difference in design between fixed and random patterns for action games. A *fixed pattern* meant that the boss would repeat the same moves every time, and the battle was more like a puzzle. Many action adventure titles build their bosses around this form of design. Even though the boss could be hit, they would take damage only after a specific condition or pattern had happened. The player cannot speed these battles along, nor can they do anything different, regardless of their expertise at the game. A *random pattern* is when the boss's attacks are pulled from set attacks, but the order that they'll attack is randomized. Bosses will usually pick the attack to use based on proximity to the player's character. In response, boss battles are more organic and require the player to be reacting constantly to the fight. Expert players know what attacks the boss will do, but they will have no idea what's coming.

Players who could react to the fight and master their available options quickly could speed through bosses like this because the boss could always be hurt. In speed-running cases, a sufficiently skilled player could actually prevent bosses from going into different phases if they know the right order to attack them.

Among action games today, the *Dark Souls* franchise is the best example of how random patterns can lead to engaging fights between the player and the bosses. Each boss fight in *DMC 3* was with a unique enemy, with its own specific patterns and strategy to deal with.

With that said, all the bosses in the game only had a few patterns, and it was easy for expert players to force the boss to repeat attacks by knowing how to engage them. The only boss that was repeated (not counting a **boss rush** section) was Dante's brother, Vergil.

Vergil showed up several times in the game as a boss for the player to go up against. However, fans probably remember the final boss fight the most.

The Vergil fight at the end of the game was one of the first real examples of how a random pattern can elevate a battle. Vergil goes through his variety of attacks, which vary from close to long-range. The big twist for the finale was Vergil activating the same Devil Trigger power that lets him do more damage and recover his health.

Beating the game required the player to get around the fact that the boss could use similar tactics, and it forced them to adapt to the changing conditions of when

Vergil goes devil. Other examples of the player fighting enemies with similar abilities would be the "Demon Ryu" fights of *Ninja Gaiden Black* and the red phantoms of the *Dark Souls* series.

The best action games, in my opinion, are those that feel more akin to the fighting genre, requiring the player to master the intricacies of combat and feel very cool doing it. When it comes to the technical side of expert play, *DMC 3* is the top game in the action genre, and a must-study for anyone wanting to see how far you can take the complexity of combat.

Shadow of the Colossus (2005; Playstation 2)
Boss-Focused Design

Shadow of the Colossus, developed by Team Ico, was already highly rated for its storytelling and awe-inspiring enemies, but I want to focus on its use of an underrated style of game design, boss-focused design, or boss rush design, is the design philosophy of building a game as a collection of boss fights—no more, no less.

Anyone who has played an action game knows that the player will be attacked by enemies large and small, with a boss fight waiting for them at the end of each stage. Boss-focused design removes all combat except against the actual bosses themselves. This has the impact of making a shorter, but more focused title, thanks to the experience being as streamlined as possible. *Shadow of the Colossus* was one of the best examples of boss-focused design.

The main character was tasked with defeating mysterious creatures in a strange land to restore the life of his lover. Unlike other boss-focused games out there,

Shadow of the Colossus featured a hub, in the form of the environment itself. Even though it was just seen as an in-between during fights, the world conveys a sense of awe to the player. The environmental design painted a land that any semblance of a culture has long since been destroyed. The only signs of former lives here was in the form of destroyed ruins in various areas.

It was one of the few examples over the years of a single-player game giving the player complete freedom to explore a world from the outset. The player had the option of exploring simply to see the sights and hunt down lizards that would enhance the grip meter (more on that shortly).

A core concept behind boss-focused game design is the fact that the player's moveset does not change over the course of play. Instead, each fight tests the player's mastery of the core gameplay loop. This is another reason why boss-focused games are on the short side—focusing on a single system limits how much you can keep creating original challenges before they start to repeat. With *Shadow of the Colossus*, every boss had specific weak points that the player had to reach.

To do so required the player to literally climb up and around the various colossi. The player's grip meter also doubled as the attack damage that the player would do. If the player held on too long, the grip meter would empty, and our hero would let go and possibly fall off. The sheer spectacle of attempting to ride these creatures in an attempt to kill them was one of the most memorable events of the PS2 generation.

Getting through a fight required the player to deal with the random actions of the colossi while trying to get at the weak points. Every battle was 100% unique, and it felt different thanks to the varying conditions. One battle took place in a lake with a flying colossus, and another in a desert, with a focus on trying to catch the colossus while riding your horse.

The boss patterns were very basic, with only a handful of possible moves that they would use depending on the player's positions. The fights themselves were always split into two parts: the player gets onto the Colossus and then works her or his way to the weak points.

Despite the varying conditions and environments, the player's abilities were never changed or altered during the 16 boss fights. Instead, each colossus emphasized or deemphasized certain aspects of the core gameplay loop. Even though the main character's horse, Agro, was the only form of transportation to the bosses, he was only used in a handful of the colossus fights. By focusing on specific aspects of the gameplay, *Shadow of the Colossus* kept each boss fight memorable and prevented the fights from all playing out the same way.

Shadow of the Colossus's world was ripe for environmental storytelling. There was very little dialogue in the game. Outside of screaming "Agro," the main character did not talk.

The world had a beauty and mysteriousness to it, as mentioned before. While the colossi never spoke, that didn't stop some players from connecting with the strange beasts and feeling sadness about their deaths. It was never brought up during the game, but the colossi never attacked the player until they engaged with him or her. This was a game where the most violent character was the supposed hero of the story. Even when everything was said and done, the game ended on a mysterious note; just like the team's previous hit, *Ico.*

Shadow of the Colossus was not a long game, and it didn't have to be. Boss-focused game design is not about padding the content with additional elements separate from the boss fights. Because of that freedom, the developers were able to turn all their attention to designing fights that never felt the same, despite the player's moveset not changing. This kind of genre exemplifies the concept of quality over quantity.

At the end of the day, good boss design is about testing the players' mastery of a game and their skill levels at different parts. The various colossi ramp up in terms of complexity and difficulty just as they would in any action title. Even though there weren't other enemies or gameplay systems for the player to use, you still need to balance your game in terms of the difficulty curve.

As with *Ico,* the story of *Shadow of the Colossus* remained mysterious throughout. Arguably, the ending didn't exactly leave you with a feeling of finality, but that went with the spirit of the game.

Shadow of the Colossus was not about the destination, but the journey. Some people rush through the game, taking on colossus after colossus, while others took the time to explore the world. Not having minor enemies to fight gave the game's pacing a different kind of ebb and flow. The players could relax, as long as they wanted before going after a colossus, and then things would ramp up during the fights.

It's fascinating to see games with supposedly required elements taken out or downplayed to create something new. *Shadow of the Colossus* and games like it showed that when it comes to video games, quality of design is more important than quantity of hours.

12

Team Fortress 2 (2007; PC and Multiple Platforms)
The Birth of Games as a Service

Team Fortress 2 is an example of a game that deserves to be studied not because of where it was at 1.0, but what happened afterward. The original *Team Fortress* became one of the standout **mods** (or modifications) for *Half-Life 1*, and possibly the first example of a class-based shooter. It would take Valve almost a decade to release the 1.0 version of *Team Fortress 2*. When it did, fans were shocked to see a completely different aesthetic used for the game. Valve replaced the gritty look of the original with a stylized, cartoonish look. While this change shocked gamers at the first reveal, this would become one of the major elements contributing toward the game's success and long-term viability over the years.

The original concept for *Team Fortress 2* was the same as the first game. Two teams of players would fight against each other, attacking and defending maps. The classes had their own strengths and weaknesses, but each one served a unique purpose. Using health and damage for balance, the classes slid into their specified roles.

The heavy had the highest level of health and could rip apart the enemy team with his mini-gun, but he was nowhere near as mobile as classes like the solider or the scout. Perhaps the most rage-inducing class was the spy, who could take the form of any player on the opposing team to deliver one-hit-kill backstabs with his knife.

Following the release of *Team Fortress 2,* Valve began to expand not just the gameplay, but the story around the characters. The *Meet the Team* video series explored the background of each of the game's nine classes, giving each one a personality and showing off the power of the source engine.

Typically, games of this kind would receive small patches here and there, and maybe some new maps. The point was that the developers were adding to what's there, not changing the core concept. Due to this development strategy, most multi-player games that weren't **MMOs** (short for Massively Multiplayer Online) games saw their player bases shrink until only the most dedicated fans were left. Many titles with online multiplayer capability during the late 1990s into the 2000s had their servers turned off once the majority of people moved on to the next game. Valve would buck that trend; in 2008, they released what would become the first major update to *Team Fortress 2.*

The Gold Rush Update added in a new gameplay mode called Payload and new achievements for the medic, and started the push toward a long-term progression system in the form of items. For the 1.0 iteration, each class in the game was fixed in terms of what they could do; in other words, every class always behaved the same way. Items changed all that and started to allow players to customize each class. Unlike other games that would go down this road, the items in *Team Fortress 2* were "side-grades"; that is, improving the player in one aspect at the cost of another.

This was a smart move by Valve because it allowed them to counter the power curve issue that **free-to-play** games face today. When you sell the player base power, it creates a system of the haves versus the have-nots. Whoever can spend the most money on the game will have the best advantage, and this can easily drive away the majority of your fan base.

The other problem with this approach is that it creates a never-ending arms race for players to try and one-up everyone else, destroying any attempt at balancing your game among the player base. Games that are about the arms race tend to drive away casual and midtier players, who have no chance of catching up to the hardcore fans who have spent the money.

The *Team Fortress 2* items never changed the built-in functionality of the class; players were never going to get a superfast, double-jumping heavy. Instead, they could tweak an aspect or play style to make it better, but that would reduce the class's effectiveness. In return, players could tweak the class to their preferred play style, but at the cost of losing class utility in an area that they may not be a fan of.

As more updates were introduced, the world of *Team Fortress 2* started to expand. It was no longer just about two teams fighting over territory, but an elaborate back story fueled by the creativeness of the art style and Valve's writing. A new update no longer just came with patch notes, but a back story and a multiday event. By going with a stylized look, *Team Fortress 2* has aged amazingly well, and it stands out among shooters to this day.

Without knowing it at the time, Valve was setting the standard of the model known as **Games as a Service**. The model has since been adopted by developers large and small—continuing to support their games to keep interest and profit growing.

Even though the basic DNA of *Team Fortress 2* remains, the game is a far different experience today than it was at launch. We also can cite *Team Fortress 2* as the first retail game released to go free to play while still successful. Today, anyone can download the game and start playing it without any upfront cost.

Instead of relying on game sales to drive profits, Valve used the addition of the in-game store and their ever-growing supply of items. You will earn random items as you play each week, but you also could spend money to acquire items directly or open loot boxes. The push and pull of time versus money has become a major element of any free-to-play game. Even though many titles favor money, you still must allow players to earn content through general play.

With enough time, players could unlock the vast majority of game-effecting items simply by playing and letting them drop. For people who wanted faster options, they could buy keys for the loot boxes or just buy the items direct through the Mann-Co store or steam trading.

In addition, *Team Fortress 2* was the first game to really open the door for **modders** to not only show off their work, but also get paid for them. Starting with the Polycount Pack and growing through the Steam workshop, modders have submitted items to Valve and the community to be voted on and hopefully implemented into *Team Fortress 2*. If a modder's item gets picked up, she or he will earn a percentage of the earnings from people who buy that item.

Team Fortress 2 has become an institution among gamers and fans. There have been annual events, more maps and game modes, and many, many hats. All the while, Valve has not added any new classes that would have dramatically changed the base gameplay. Some have argued that the game is a lot messier now with all the new options and modes, but it has been a small price to pay for its continued success. When it comes to the potential and impact of Games as a Service, *Team Fortress 2* is the undisputed poster child for what that feature can do for a game.

13

The World Ends with You (2007; Nintendo DS)

Thinking Way Outside the Box

When people think of Square Enix, they associate the megadeveloper/publisher with the Japanese role-playing game (or **JRPG**) genre. *Final Fantasy* and *Kingdom Hearts* may be well loved around the world, but for my money, my favorite game from the studio is *The World Ends with You* (*TWEWY*).

We could dedicate an entire book to the unique design of *TWEWY*, not just one section (but this will do for now). Combat relied on controlling two different characters, one on each screen. The main character, Neku, was controlled using the touch screen on the bottom, while a second character used XABY or the D-Pad and was viewed in the top screen.

How all the elements of the interface came together was that Neku and his partner had different rules that controlled how they fought the enemies. Neku used pins that were activated by touch-based controls. One pin, which brings a spike out of the ground, required the player to swipe upward with the stylus. Also, Neku could be moved around the field while his partner remained stationary.

On the top screen, the partner had a minigame-style system that granted more damage based on the player's input. One character attacked by playing a game of high and low with cards. Unlike Neku, the partner could only use a defensive action and did not move around the field.

To create a sense of flow, the two characters shared a single health bar (and the same enemies as well) and a magical orb that they pass between them. Whoever was holding the orb did more damage with their attacks, and this was designed to give the player something to focus on during combat. Players always should focus, offensive-wise, on the character holding the orb and do their best to dodge attacks with the other character.

In terms of story, the entire game took place in a heightened version of the Shibuya district of Japan, with one of the most amazing soundtracks in a video game. *TWEWY* is one of only a handful of RPGs that took place in a modern-day world, as opposed to fantasy or sci-fi.

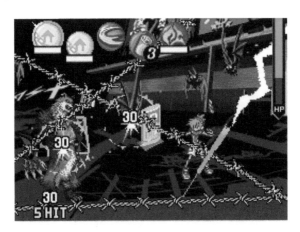

Neku had been killed, and his only chance to come back to life was to play a game with other killed individuals against the makers of the game. Each chapter had the player teaming up with a different character, while unlocking new systems and challenges.

What made the game worthy of study was how every single mechanic and system differed from its peers in the genre and worked in a controlled-chaos kind of way. Starting with the gear, each piece of clothing came with a unique bonus effect that could be used only if the store owner liked the player enough to reveal it after spending enough money. The shops in Shibuya range from clothing for teens to luxury stores with their own unique stock of items.

Clothing required a bravery stat that goes up through play and levels up, to simulate the idea of someone wearing weird clothing to them. While normal shirts and socks could be worn easily, high-fashion or more exotic clothing would be a harder sell. Continuing with that thought, the player could influence the fashion styles of an area, which would increase or decrease the player's abilities depending on what items the player's character was wearing. These changes were important, as Neku's pins were also attached to the various fashion styles. Using pins that were in season would give them an attack boost compared to ones that weren't.

The player could eat food that provided permanent benefits to her or his character, as long as there was room to eat for that day. Food was "digested" after each battle, and when it was fully digested, the player got the enhancement. The various pins would evolve based on how the player earned experience with them. That's right: There were different ways of earning experience based on fighting enemies, returning to the game after an extended period, and other actions.

One of my favorite elements was that the game lets players sculpt the difficulty to their choosing. There were three ways for players to alter the difficulty in the game: choosing how many fights to have in a row, the overall difficulty of the game, and how much max health to turn off.

The more fights that players did at once would give them a multiplier toward money and experience. The overall difficulty determined the enemy's stats and how aggressive they were. In turn, it would determine what items the enemy could drop after the fight was over. Most enemies had possible item drops for fighting them on each difficulty level, and the higher-tiered items would not drop unless the player set the difficulty to one of the harder settings. Finally, for every chosen drop to the max health pool, the player would raise the drop rate of items after each fight.

Getting the best gear and drops in the game required players to not only make the game harder, but figure out how much to lower their health while still being able to survive the fight.

The beauty of this system was that it allowed players to play the game at their own pace, but at the same time, reward those who wanted to challenge themselves. Too often, designers will struggle with how to balance the difficulty of a game properly. Sometimes they'll make it too hard and turn off newcomers, or they'll make it too easy and core gamers will not want to sit through it.

By letting players control the difficulty in such a way, they were always given the final say in how easy or hard the game would be at any time. Players could play through the game for the story completely on the easiest setting, or they could see everything at the highest difficulty level. The game would accommodate all players, no matter what skill level they had. Lesser-skilled players were able to play through the game just fine with what was available to them. For those willing to make the game harder, they were rewarded with more options and abilities to compensate for the enhanced difficulty, but neither group was punished for playing the game their way.

Even with all the systems added, the developers saw fit to add a separate minigame built around a fictional game of spinning tops built on using your pins and additional challenges after the main story was finished. Everything worked together despite how unique all the systems were.

The dual-screen nature of the Nintendo DS afforded designers to get really creative with their designs, and *TWEWY* was one of the best of these. The game was designed from the ground up to make full use of this setup, but attempts to export it to other platforms have not worked due to the unique control scheme and UI.

TWEWY may not have been a big seller for Square Enix, but it nevertheless remains one of its most ambitious titles. If you want to experience a JRPG like no other, definitely give it a shot.

Left 4 Dead (2008; PC, Xbox 360, and Mac)

(Co-op) Friends to the Very End

FPSs have always been about the competitive aspect of playing against each other, with the likes of *Doom, Unreal,* and many more. To help spice things up, many third-person shooters and FPSs have been bundled with **co-op** modes; along with fan-made games like *Natural Selection* and *Killing Floor*. Famous **AAA** examples would be the zombie and horde modes of the *Call of Duty* and *Gears of War* series respectively. While these modes can be a lot of fun, they are usually considered secondary to the multiplayer experience of the player-versus-player design.

Getting a full game built on cooperative gameplay is a rare treat, and why *Left 4 Dead* was such a surprise. Developed by Turtle Rock Studios, *Left 4 Dead* was designed as a whole game built around co-op. Four players had to survive against infected people turned into rage-filled monsters. Each campaign was framed around moving through a specific area, trying to find your way to the next safe room, and ultimately to get rescued.

The beauty of *Left 4 Dead*'s design came down to a simple tenet: No one was above the group. A popular mainstay of skill-based games is the fact that a good-enough player could outshine the rest of the people playing—but not in *Left 4 Dead*.

Turtle Rock's answer to the "one-man army" came in the form of the special infected. These enemies were explicitly designed to separate and take the team apart. The Hunter and Smoker would incapacitate a player, who then would have to be rescued. Boomers would explode upon dying or vomit on players that partially blinded them and summoned other common infected. Finally, the tank was just an all-powerful brute that requires multiple gunshots to be taken down.

The one infected who was unique was the witch. One witch could spawn on any map and would become aggressive if fired on, or if the survivors got too close. When triggered, the witch could incapacitate a survivor in one hit before trying to finish her or him off.

Once players were incapacitated, their only hope was for a second player or players to come and pick them up. This also had the side effect of further making the groups stronger than the individual. Even losing just one survivor during a level meant that the survivors would be outnumbered by the special infected.

Operating as a well-oiled machine was the only way to survive in *Left 4 Dead*, and this was expanded on with the game's versus mode. The versus mode put two teams of four against each other, with one playing the survivors and the other as the special infected. Both sides would play the same map once as each group before moving through the campaign. The concept was to score points based on how far the survivor team would progress through the level and how many survived at the end.

Playing as the special infected once again brought in the focus of teamwork. Alone, the special infected were easily countered, but a well-coordinated strike was another matter entirely. Each special infected played differently, requiring players to master four different kinds of characters.

As the hunter, the player was usually the first one to act as a distraction for the other infected. Smokers had to be sneaky to grab the most vulnerable player, or pull someone off a ledge. A good boomer could make or break the attack, by causing a horde to spawn and sow chaos among the survivors. When a tank was spawned, one player at random was chosen to control it. A player-controlled tank could be a nightmare to take out, as they could coordinate with the remaining special infected much easier compared to the AI. The only infected that wasn't playable was the witch, but she could still spawn on the map and be used as a trap for the special infected.

A versus match came to a head on each of the finale levels. The survivors had to survive against multiple waves (and tanks) until help came. With the survivors stuck in one area, the special infected team had to work even harder to deal with the survivors. The second game would expand on the finales by requiring the surviving team to sometimes perform specific tasks between the waves.

While there were single-player options to play *Left 4 Dead* with AI bots, this was an experience meant for a group of friends. The AI simply could not coordinate with the other players at the same level as other human players.

The game's AI Director deserves a special shout-out. The director's job was to manage the experience of the game based on the difficulty and how well the survivors were doing. Resources like grenades and healing items would be dispersed in select areas of the game space. The director also would spawn in the special infected and bring in hordes. Sadly, the idea of having a virtual dungeon master did not go far enough to make each play feel different.

Outside of a few levels, there was always one specific way through and several hard-coded chokepoints. For expert players in versus, they would know what areas to run through and could punish a poor infected team by not giving them the chance to make a proper attack.

Left 4 Dead was one of the best examples of how to design a cooperative game and to make sure that everyone was working together. *Left 4 Dead*'s sequel would add more special infected to continue their role as group breakers, but the horror theme of the original felt more focused than in *Left 4 Dead 2*. With that said, some of the best multiplayer matches I had involved playing with the *Left 4 Dead 2* additions on the original's maps.

In *Left 4 Dead 2*, the special infected options were enhanced with the addition of the spitter, charger, and jockey. Valve looked at the general play of *Left 4 Dead* and saw that it focused on the survivors camping in a defendable position. A skilled team of survivors could hunker down in one area and prevent even the best team of special infected from being able to do anything.

With *Left 4 Dead 2*, the aim of the new special infected was to ruin camping while still providing new special infected strategies. The jockey could leap on a survivor's back and maneuver her or him off ledges or simply away from the group. The spitter left a puddle of acid that did more damage the longer someone stood in it. Finally, the charger punished rushers by knocking them back and stunned survivors when he charged into them.

By expanding the number of special infected, it made playing as them more varied than before. Having a pool of six to pick among (not counting the tank or witch) offered greater flexibility to special infected teams. Now, either a boomer or a spitter could be used to create chaos for the survivors. Advanced play was built around tag-team combos, such as the charger knocking survivors back into a spitter pool or the jockey leading players into a smoker or hunter trap. The added benefit of special infected explicitly designed to fight against camping made replaying the *Left 4 Dead* maps more challenging.

Left 4 Dead 2 was also an attempt by Valve to bring in storytelling outside of the game, similar to *Team Fortress 2*. Several comics were written and additional maps were added after the game's release. A horde survival mode was eventually folded into the multiplayer, but most fans preferred versus mode.

Multiplayer doesn't automatically have to mean competition, and cooperative design can lead to unique forms of game design. Whether you had four or eight friends, *Left 4 Dead* was a great experience.

15

Spelunky (2008; PC, and Multiple Platforms)
Procedural Platforming

The rogue-like genre has exploded in the last decade among indie developers, thanks to the focus on difficulty and replayability. Traditional rogue-likes were built with RPG stats and designed as a turn-based experience. With that said, we have seen some amazing exceptions, such as the one we're about to discuss. *Spelunky* was one of the first games to not only show how far you could push the rogue-like genre, but also the power of **procedural generation**.

Spelunky's main gameplay loop was built around platforming. How well the player could navigate the ever-changing levels (more on that in a minute) would determine whether he or she lived or died. The story had the player searching a mysterious temple for a great treasure, with traps, enemies, and even gravity getting in the way. The controls and UI were finely tuned to make sure that the player always had control of the character.

From a basic gameplay standpoint, the player could run, jump, use a whip for attacking, and had two basic items. Bombs could be thrown to destroy most enemies and obstacles, while ropes would allow the player to climb up or down safely.

As with rogue-likes, *Spelunky* featured an assortment of items that, at their worst, provided advantages while playing, and at their best broke the game. Understanding the application of the items afforded the player with a lot more utility than just using the game's basic items of bombs and rope.

Advanced play of *Spelunky* revolved around players making use of the additional items to supplement their ability. Despite how maneuverable a player was at the beginning, she or he could gain the ability to jet-pack around, wield a shotgun, and more.

Spelunky was one of the more skill-intensive rogue-likes released. The player started with three points of health, and while that helped for normal enemies, there were plenty of ways to die. Spikes, carnivorous plants, lava, and even just falling from really high up could end the player's life. Lucky runs could last over 30 minutes, while unlucky ones could end in 30 seconds.

In order to keep the player motivated to continue playing when death was around every corner, there has to be a way to make sure that the game feel fresh. To do that, *Spelunky* featured one of the best uses of procedural generation in any video game.

Procedural generation is about designing the engine of your game to create original content during play, guaranteeing that the player would never run into the same exact experience twice. Each level of the game was built literally from top to bottom by the game engine, making sure that every play was completely different. Not only that, but the procedural generation was good enough to make a level that was beatable and consistent in environmental design.

There is a big difference between good and bad procedural generation. Many lesser games create levels that feel right at home in an M. C. Escher painting. *Spelunky*'s level designs had the look and play of something handmade; which in of itself is worthy of being studied. After enough plays, experts could start to see the blueprint design of the levels, but that didn't make them any less unique. Designer Derek Yu talked about designing the algorithm on his site and about giving the engine specific-enough instructions to create a consistent form, while still being open enough to keep the levels from being too similar.

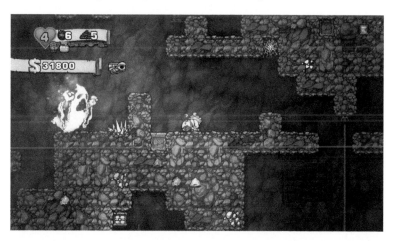

Procedural generation comes down to having the algorithm (i.e., set of instructions followed by the computer) be flexible enough to create a variety of content, but still constricted, so that there is a set foundation for generation. In the game, the player would always appear at the top part of a level, with the exit always somewhere at the bottom of the stage.

No matter how the level was generated, the instructions within the algorithm made sure that there was a valid way to get through the stage based on the player's skill level alone.

The game was split into several environmental biomes: Temple, Jungle, Ice, Tomb, and Hell (which was a hidden area). The biome tells the computer what kind of enemies, aesthetics, environmental hazards, and possible events to use when generating a level. An expert player knew what to expect in terms of content, but never in terms of the structure of the level.

Spelunky's procedural generation worked hand in hand with the platformer gameplay to present a rogue-like that wasn't built on RPG progression. Due to the focus on the player's skill, the architecture of the levels in itself was enough to provide a difference experience each time, compared to an RPG, which is more about items and events.

In an RPG setting, a player who is skilled enough can figure out the best optimization on how to play and get around any challenges. *Spelunky*'s design

---

meant that you always had to be at your best to succeed. A run could end in victory or on the very first level, depending on the knowledge and skill of the player.

Spelunky was one of the first games to implement rogue-like design outside of a pure RPG, paving the way for games like *The Binding of Isaac* and *FTL*. The thrill and ever-present danger of death were easily translated to the game, along with the expert angle. As the player's understanding of the game grew, how she or he would approach each level would change.

Advanced tactics involved finding hidden areas and dealing with shopkeepers to load up on equipment and items. For the truly brave, you could perform the requirements needed to access the game's hidden final world in Hell. Reaching Hell tasked players to picking up specific items within each area, and the Hell biome featured the hardest obstacles and enemies.

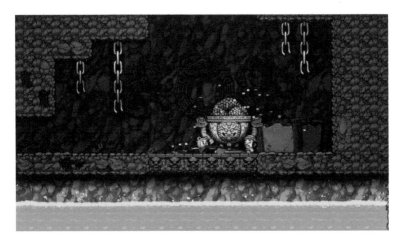

Even though the difficulty of the play would change based on what levels were generated, expert players were able to use their knowledge at the game to mitigate the challenge. In some cases, they could even make the game harder for themselves by attempting to go for a high score or completing harder events when they appeared.

One final point that needs to be mentioned was on the inclusion of a daily run mode. A daily run is where every player is given the same seed, or a copy of a generated run to play. You are given only one chance to run through it, and players are ranked based on their score. The addition of this competitive mode added even more replayability to *Spelunky*, thanks to giving players a way to see who the best was for that day. The mode is so popular that it has become a standard feature for rogue-like games.

The thrill of a rogue-like isn't just for RPGs anymore. With the right design and replayability, even something as simple as a two-dimensional (2D) platformer could be played for months and keep the player engaged. The very fact that people are still playing the game today and running into original-level designs is proof of the impact that procedural generation can have on replayability.

16

Demon's Souls (2009; Playstation 3)
The Action Rogue-Like

Demon's Souls shook up the industry, to the point of defining titles before and after its release. FromSoftware had been around as a company for over 30 years at that point, and it had made a number of great, but niche successes. The game that I most remembered them for pre–*Demon's Souls* was *Armored Core*. During their time in the 1990s, they created a RPG series called *King's Field*, which would become the precursor to *Demon's Souls*.

King's Field set the foundation for what was to come: a focus on melee combat, mazelike levels, and of course, extreme difficulty. The series met with a mixed reception, and only a few of the games were officially released in the United States.

In 2009, FromSoftware planned on releasing *Demon's Souls* only in Japan and Asia, but the immense reception that the game received convinced the Japanese publisher/developer Atlus to bring the game to the United States. Early previews and impressions out of Japan convinced U.S. gamers that this was a game to check out. In fact, this was the game that convinced me to buy a PS3, as well as buying a copy of the game three months before I actually got the system.

Demon's Souls featured the DNA of *King's Field*, but it was greatly expanded upon in both depth and design. Taking place in the third person rather than the first, the game was built on a focus on real-time combat. The switch to third person also allowed players an easier time with situational awareness compared to *King's Field*.

The combat system, now antiquated by its spiritual sequels, was a revelation for action and RPG fans at the time. Combat took place in real time, with a focus on positioning and movement. Longer weapons had a greater range, but the players needed to watch where they were swinging them in relation to the walls around them. Instead of being built around one weapon type or style, the game had numerous weapon and armor types to use.

From daggers to giant swords, players were free to use whatever strategies and gear they could find to get through the game. The three broad categories of play were focused on melee, ranged, and/or spell casting. Gear also could be upgraded at the two blacksmiths in the game. Upgrades not only required players to purchase them, but they had to have the necessary materials. Upgrading gear provided players with the most visible improvement to their characters—increasing their ability to deal and receive damage.

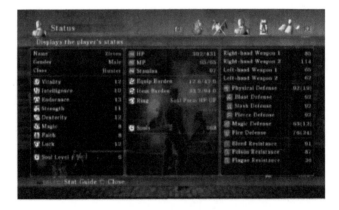

Gear and builds were the areas where the RPG side of *Demon's Souls* took over. Players could use gear only if they had enough points in the respective stat to use it. In turn, players were pushed towards different styles of play. While the game had classes, they would only determine the starting load-out and stats; it was up to players to define how they wanted to play. So long as they met the stat requirements, players could decide to be a sneaky sorcerer, a mighty warrior who could cast blessings, and many more characters.

The stats also had the passive benefit of improving a player's character and making him or her better overall. The leveling system itself included a progressively growing cost based on the character's level in order to add another stat point. This allowed rapid character progress early in the game, but which slowed down into the middle and end of the game.

The use of a stamina meter was one of the major dividing points between the *Souls* series and a traditional action game. Blocking, dodging, running, and attacking would consume stamina. Running out of stamina during a fight meant that players couldn't attack or defend themselves, leaving them wide open to the myriad of enemies.

Tying everything together was a brilliant risk versus reward system inspired by the rogue-like genre. Anyone who has played a rogue-like knows that one of the core pillars is the extreme punishment for dying. When a player died, all progress was wiped out, and the player returned to the start. The reason why this was fine was that every new play featured a completely different world to explore.

Demon's Souls, and future games in the Souls-Like genre, would meet in the middle. The level designs themselves were all hard-coded and fixed, with no random or procedural generation in effect. Upon dying, the player was returned to the start of the level, and all enemies were revived. By opening up shortcuts in the level, the player would begin to make permanent progress. The risk came into play with what the player lost when they died. Souls earned from killing enemies were both currency and experience points in the world of *Demon's Souls*. Upon death, the player dropped all the souls that she or he possessed on the ground. If the player did not recover them before dying again, they were lost forever.

This created an interesting dynamic of always questioning how far to push things before returning to the game's hub to spend your souls. Every fight could turn into a bloodbath for players who weren't prepared. With this system in place, *Demon's Souls* would have the punishment of a rogue-like, but featured handmade levels that players were happy to live, die, and repeat over and over again.

Speaking of the levels, each of the game's five worlds featured some of the best level designs for the time. The world would provide the player with unique environmental hazards, enemies to fight, and of course, secrets to uncover. The levels were an enemy onto themselves against the player, featuring death traps and plenty of bottomless pits to fall into.

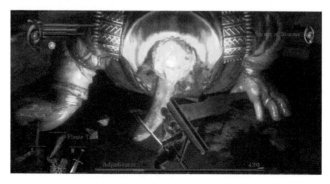

One of the reasons why *Demon's Souls* was chosen for this first book was due to the structure of the game. With each world being its own ecosystem, that made it easier for players to compartmentalize the various environments and build a mental map of the game space. The future *Souls* titles went with an open-world structure, which was far more ambitious, but it had a different feel than *Demon's Souls*.

As the player, you could easily track your progress through *Demon's Souls*, and with each world being separate from one another, it made it easier for the designers to keep everything focused. There was less downtime moving from one locale to the other, with each level being its own personal dungeon of pain for the player to explore.

Besides the environmental storytelling that went into the design of each world, the various enemies that were unique to the worlds helped to give them a greater sense of personality. This was expanded further by the variety of normal and boss-class enemies.

All manner of enemies were put into the game to test the player. There were commoners who would rush the player while frantically slashing, to skeletons that would cartwheel around the battlefield. Mastering the game required the player to slow down and figure out the kinds of attacks that the enemies would use. Taking things further, the bosses would become a staple of the *Souls* series, both for their design and challenge.

Every boss fight was with a completely different encounter that tested the player in a unique way. Some examples were the colossal Tower Knight, and the tag-team battle of the Maneaters. These bosses would exemplify one of the cornerstones of Souls-Likes: The player must be prepared for anything.

As we discussed earlier in this book with *Devil May Cry 3*, the *Souls* series would become the poster child for random-pattern boss design. The player had to respond to the unique touches of the boss with the build of his or her choosing. Not one boss in the entirety of *Demon's Souls* repeated either the design or situation of another battle. Players had to react to whatever the boss would throw at them during a battle, as one wrong move could lead to death.

The online component of *Demon's Souls* would also become another famous part of the game's design—the way that it combined co-op, **PVP**, and fostered the community all at once. Playing online, you could read and leave messages at specific parts in the world for other players. Sometimes they were tricks, sometimes they were funny, and sometimes they pointed to hidden areas. The game's risk versus reward aspect would come into play with online interactions.

When the player died, they entered "spirit form," where they had less max health but could not be attacked by players. Spirits could join other players who were in "human form" to help them fight and regain their bodies. While in human form, players had their full health bar available, but also became targets for invading players to kill them for rewards.

As another element of the world building and community side of *Demon's Souls*, players who were online could interact with bloodstains on the ground to see the last few seconds of a player who died there. There was always this sense of the entire community trying to complete the challenge that the game presented.

Our final point to make in this chapter was another aspect that the *Souls* series has become famous for: an elaborate lore and backstory that was completely optional to the gameplay. After the initial cutscene, there were very few breaks to deliver exposition to the players. What the designers did was place all the lore elements onto every (and I do mean *every*) item in the game. Clothing from specific characters would go into detail about their backstory. Even the souls that the players earned from the bosses would explore how these enemies came to be.

None of the lore was required to play through the game, but it provided a rich tapestry that players have been piecing together throughout the entire series. If a player wanted to explore how these lands came to be, or were just there to see "Target was destroyed," the game accommodated that.

Demon's Souls paved the way for a new kind of design, as a middle ground between rogue-likes and traditional action games. Since the release of it and *Dark Souls*, Souls-Like has become a popular subgenre in the game industry. Perhaps even more important, *Demon's Souls* was considered the first attempt to bring challenging games back to the mainstream industry. The *Souls* series would go on to be described as "tough, but fair," and that would be a completely different discussion we could have.

Demon's Souls, and later games in the series, are must-plays for anyone who wants to see how to balance difficulty and fairness to the player.

17

Plants vs. Zombies (2009; PC and Multiple Platforms)

The Ultimate Hardcore Casual Game

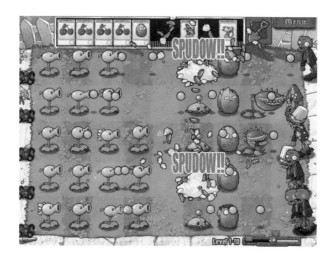

Casual game design is frowned upon by a lot of hardcore gamers, who say that it's easy to create something simple, but that can't be further from the truth. Creating a casual game is about designing an experience that provides entertainment without requiring a high skill to enjoy. The best casual game designers know that their audience will include people who are familiar with the genre as well as those who have never encountered it before.

Of the many casual game companies in the world, only a few have managed to elevate casual design. *Plants vs. Zombies*, by Popcap, is easily the company's best and most recognizable game, and an example of how to do casual games right.

The game's core gameplay loop was built around tower defense. The player's job was to defend your home from waves of zombies coming to get her or him. The defenses came in the form of a wide variety of plants that had various effects, attacks, and utilities. As the game went on, new zombies and plants were introduced, along with new conditions like nighttime and defending a pool that limited plant placement.

Surviving each stage required the player to use basic tower defense strategy. Sunflowers were the game's resource generator, and the player typically built at least four per map. The zombies would attack in any of the lanes, and the player had to build up defenses properly. Zombies would have different health values or did something special on the field. For example, there was a zombie using a pogo stick to jump over the first plant he came to.

What made *Plants vs. Zombies* work had more to do with what was under the surface of the gameplay. First, there was a streamlined UI designed for anyone to be able to figure out. The creator of *Plants vs. Zombies,* George Fan, talked about the work that went into the UI for a **GDC** presentation. The game's UI was designed to catch the player's attention and focus it on how to learn the game, whether the player was a fan of the genre, or in Fan's case, his mother. The game's opening levels did an amazing job of easing new players into the situation and giving them an understanding of the rules.

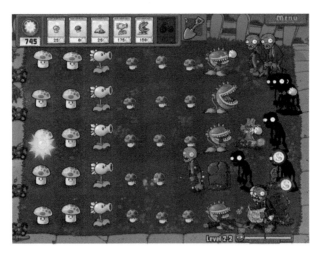

Everything in the game, from how the elements were placed on the UI to the shape of the icons, was iterated upon to allow for maximum understanding. The simple act of making sure that the player would build sunflowers first took the team several tries to make that lesson perfectly clear. So much about the game's UI may have been taken for granted by expert players who quickly adapted to the game, but it was essential in expanding the audience.

The stage flow also deserved to be called out for pacing and progression. The game's various chapters were all designed around an escalating complexity curve. While the gameplay didn't change all that much, each stage introduced something new for the player to keep track of. One of the smartest moves was the fact that beating a stage always gave the player a new reward—either a game mode or a new plant. The simple act of keeping rewards coming was a great motivator for a player.

To make sure that the audience was not growing bored, the developers introduced changes of pace at the halfway point and end of each chapter. These breaks took the form of minigames that would not be played in the same way as the regular levels.

The player still saw zombies attacking, but the act of defending was different. One stage had the player "bowling" zombies over instead of setting up defenses. The final stage in every chapter, except the end, had the player putting plants down as they would appear on a conveyor belt instead of needing resources.

Another major element that kept both new and old fans invested was a persistent system of upgrading your tools. In Crazy Dave's store, the player could unlock upgraded versions of plants, gain the ability to take more plants into a mission, and more. The player earned money via the bonus modes (which we'll talk about shortly), beating the stages, and sometimes as random drops by killing zombies.

The persistent system's impact was twofold. For new players, it allowed them to get an advantage if they were having trouble beating a level. They could buy additional defenses that would stop the zombies if their defenses were breached. For experts, it opened up new options and tactics to aid them. Advanced plants would improve the utility and was essential for taking on some of the harder challenges.

From a graphics standpoint, *Plants vs. Zombies* was a great example of style over substance. No one could say that the game was graphically intensive, but the style made it immediately recognizable. Popcap went with a cartoon design to help distract from the obvious horror connotations of having zombies come

---

at the player. Instead of people being scared by the zombies, they became a major part of the branding, along with the various plants. Even when the series spun off into three dimensions (3D) with the Garden Warfare brand, the characters were still instantly recognizable.

As the game went on, more side content was introduced to allow players a chance to take a break from the main gameplay. The first mode was a collection of challenges that took the gameplay and turned it on its head. One stage had the player fighting zombies who had plants for heads, another was a game of hide and seek with vases.

The next mode was a Zen garden where players could spend their coins to grow the various plants. By checking up on the plants and keeping them happy, you could earn far more money than just playing the game. There was also a tree where players could buy special fertilizer, with the promise of secrets as a price.

Finally, *Plants vs. Zombies* was one of a few casual games that featured a new game + option. The new game + mode mixed up the zombies in each level and randomly chose what plants the player had access to on any given level.

This all added up to a game that was designed for the casual audience but featured enough content to keep core players engaged. *Plants vs. Zombies* is one of the best games around, not just in the casual space.

18

The Binding of Isaac (2011; PC and other Platforms)

Perfected Persistence

Game designer Edmund McMillen may have had his breakout hit with *Super Meat Boy*, but *The Binding of Isaac* was more ambitious in terms of game design. Combining the creator's trademark of disturbing-looking characters and stories, the game managed to take a simple design and elevate it in ways that other designers have been chasing for years.

The story was loosely based on the biblical story of the same name. One day, Isaac's mother heard the voice of God ordering her to sacrifice Isaac. To escape, Isaac entered their basement, which acts as the dungeon for the game.

The visual design of the game was both striking and polarizing. Even though the game had a cartoon look, there was a strong focus on gross-out humor and body horror, along with the religious overtones. Isaac literally attacked his enemies by shooting his tears at them.

Isaac's movements and shooting were controlled via twin-stick controls. The game's isometric perspective was right out of the original *Legend of Zelda*, even down to the simple mapping system. The player's options in the dungeon were limited to attacking, placing bombs, and using items that could be found.

The basic gameplay of Isaac was on the simple side, but what McMillen did to keep the game replayable is why it's on this list. The game featured a different kind of procedural generation. Each room in the game was explicitly handmade, but the levels were built by combining these rooms into different layouts. The algorithm for level generation was important because it gave the player a different but still standardized level. As the player, you would always expect one treasure room, one boss room, and one shop on all the regular levels of the game.

Each biome would take up two levels in the game and had its own rooms in the generator pool to use, along with the chance of spawning specialty rooms that provided unique benefits. Advanced play involved using special rooms to exploit for maximum use. One such example was using a room that dropped money and combined it with items that spawned other items when the money was picked up to fill up on the specified item. The set rooms allowed for control and balance over the difficulty and pacing of each stage. At the same time, there was variety based on what the player found.

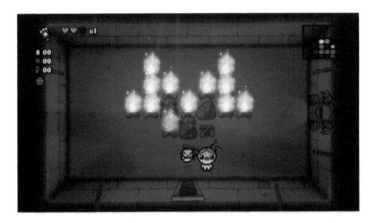

While the player's ability to control Isaac did not change, the progression curve over a single run was built on finding treasures. You could get a treasure from item shops, find the treasure room, beat the floor's boss, and in other secret ways. Every treasure in Isaac did two things: It changed Isaac's appearance and altered his abilities in some way.

Isaac, along with other characters who could be unlocked, was rated in the following categories: Health, Attack Damage, Attack Speed, Projectile Speed,

Movement Speed, and Luck. Each treasure would affect one or more attributes upon pickup.

A treasure could give Isaac more health but weaker attacks, give his shot a spread effect, or even give him a literal death laser. The key point about these treasures was that they worked on a modifier basis. It's common in games that feature a lot of items to have them replace or supersede previous upgrades.

Normally if you found a power that gave you a double shot, and then another that gave you a triple shot, the latter would replace the former because it was more powerful. This was to keep the player's power in balance and avoid the player essentially breaking the balance of the game.

In *Isaac*, however, every item would become a part of the player's plan and "stack" for the rest of the play-through. Instead of being designed around checks and balances, *Isaac*'s progression was designed to keep adding to the character's stats with no limit. This led to vastly different runs depending on the items that the player found. Combine the item that turns your default attack into bombs with the triple spread shot power and the death laser, and the player gets triple-exploding, death-laser bombs.

The number of game-affecting changes made it impossible to completely balance *The Binding of Isaac*, but that was the point. Too often, in rogue-like-designed games, the designers try to balance all the player's options so that she or he would not become too powerful. The issue is that given the randomized nature of rogue-like design, it's impossible to predict accurately what the player will get in any given run. If the player's options are too weak, it can lead to only a select number of ways to actually win.

In *Isaac*, the player could have runs where nothing, not even the game's ultimate final boss, could stop him or her. Upgrades could vary from being simple stat upgrades to run-changing effects (for better or worse). Given all the ways to grow *Isaac*, McMillen came up with a simple but elegant system to keep the game growing.

The very majority of items were locked at the start under the game's Secrets menu. As players went through the game, they would unlock secrets by completing simple and complicated tasks. A secret could be as simple as beating a boss or as complicated as getting a specific set of items over the course of a single run. Each secret would give the player something new that would appear in subsequent runs.

Besides unlocking new items, beating the game multiple times would unlock new enemy types, boss variants, and even new stages. While rogue-likes are meant to be replayed, getting the real ending in *Isaac* required multiple play-throughs to unlock the final set of levels. Even with that said, through updates and expansions, there are now even more final stages and endings for players to find. The amount of persistence in *The Binding of Isaac* helped to make it a very replayable game.

The unlocks were also an important point of gating the player and changing the game. New players would not be able to access the harder stages or even know that they existed. One of the modifiers rewarded people who kept beating the game by making everything harder.

How this was done was twofold. With the harder difficulty, fewer healing and consumable items would spawn in the levels. An important detail about *Isaac*'s procedural generation was the fact that enemy placements were not locked in specific rooms. When the game got harder, the game would unlock special variants of the enemies and was more likely to pick more difficult enemies when generating the levels.

You couldn't just make the game harder for yourself; you had to earn the privilege. For expert players, there was a huge difference in playing a new run of *Isaac* after hours of play versus just starting out. That was a big motivator to keep playing the game, despite how simple the actual gameplay was.

Despite spending over a hundred hours playing through *Isaac* and its remakes, I never once had the exact same run; this was due to the sheer number of items and their impacts. Lesser games would have only a few ways of modifying the player's ability during a run. What usually happened was that the players knew what the best items for success were and based their attempt on getting those specific items.

Going back to the limited number of successful outcomes, these titles became very repetitive, with the knowledge that if the player didn't get X, Y, or Z, they had no hope of winning. In *Isaac*, there were so many items that it became impossible to truly force a set build to play with. Not even having advanced options to reroll items and floors made it possible to get a fixed outcome.

More important, I never felt that I had to get the best items to have a chance at winning when I started playing. Some of the most exciting runs were caused by a potluck of random items, which made me have to figure out how to make lemonade out of lemons.

Normally, rogue-likes that feature set rooms could end up being repetitive over time. The reason for this is that if a player learns how to handle room X, then she or he will just repeat the strategy every time. The beauty of randomly choosing and assigning items and enemies meant that the player never knows what the right strategy will be.

Would players use powerful but slow shots, or weak, rapid-fire attacks, or some kind of crazy build that came together in the 11th hour to utterly decimate the enemies?

The big takeaway from *Isaac* was that procedural generation, applied just right in your design, could create a title that may be simple to play but provide endless entertainment. Despite *Isaac* now being over seven years old, there hasn't been another game yet that has managed to get the **persistence systems** as right as this game does.

19

Infinifactory (2015; PC)
Emergent Puzzle Design

The use of puzzles in video games has been one of the more fascinating parts of game design over the years. While puzzle design in the traditional sense started out as a part of adventure games, it has since become its own genre.

We could easily fill another book discussing some of the most interesting or unique puzzle games in the game industry, as the term *puzzle* can mean vastly different designs and require thought processes to solve them. Puzzles can be abstract and focus on logic challenges, or they can focus on the environment and the player's comprehension of the world.

The key limitation of most puzzles in video games was that they were designed around a "lock and key" philosophy. Popularized by early adventure games like *Maniac Mansion* and *King's Quest*, lock-and-key puzzles are built around a fixed problem and solution. The lock represents what's stopping the player from moving forward, and the key is the item or choice that the player needs to solve it.

Once the player finds out what the game wants from them, the puzzle is forever solved. In this way, even the most celebrated puzzles or adventure games in the game industry can only truly be experienced one time by the player. Due to the linear nature of these puzzles, many adventure/puzzle designers created esoteric solutions that would require a lot of trial and error (or dumb luck) on the player's part. The 1990s was the first golden age of the adventure genre, but even the best franchises had some insane puzzle solutions, such as the infamous "mustache cat" of *Gabriel Knight* that forced players to figure out a solution that made no logical sense.

Even though the adventure genre has dialed back the crazy puzzles, they are still designed around linear solutions to this day. With all that said, one developer who has been doing things differently is Zach Barth of Zachtronics. Their first big success and claim to fame was *Spacechem*, a game that disguised programming logic puzzles with chemistry. Each of his games has followed a similar modus operandi when it comes to the puzzle design.

The puzzles in a Zachtronic game are not your standard lock-and-key puzzles, despite having set start and end points. The complexity of a Zachtronic puzzle was in creating a solution that satisfied the demand of the puzzle. The player was always given a set of tools and options that could be combined in intentional (or unintentional) ways. The tools that the player was given had a fixed purpose but offered flexibility when combined with each other.

There was never only one solution to any of the puzzles; instead, players were rated on how optimized their solutions were within specific categories, and then the solutions were ranked by the other players. All the puzzles were built on the internal logic of the game, not on outside knowledge. This was how the puzzles from Zachtronics essentially "hid" the programming logic by the **abstraction** of the game space.

The reason why we're discussing *Infinifactory* is that it is the first (for now) game from Zachtronics to use this kind of emergent puzzle design in a 3D space. The story had the player being abducted one night and put to work creating assembly lines for a mysterious alien race.

Every tool in *Infinifactory* took the form of a block that performed some kind of function. Simple examples would be conveyor blocks that could move objects. After a few puzzles, the game would start to train the player to combine blocks in specific ways to create minimachines. One block allowed the player to create logic gates to set up physical if/then statements that could be combined for performing specific acts.

Each block had the utility to be used in different ways by a creative player. A player could use the shape of an object to trigger specific logic gates that would send the object to different parts of the assembly line. The idea was that the player should not think in terms of one giant machine/solution, but instead in individual segments designed to perform a specific function that were all combined into the final solution.

Due to the machines taking up physical space within *Infinifactory*, the game was a lot easier to process than the abstraction of Zachtronic's previous titles. Players could see in real time how objects were interacting with their machines and made adjustments accordingly. Any programmer knows that when you're building a program, it can be very hard to tell if there is a breakdown in the logic. With *Infinifactory*, on the other hand, any breakdowns could be immediately seen, and a solution could be devised.

The ability to craft solutions or come up with new elements is an example of **emergent game design**. Creating the conditions for emergent gameplay requires an expert understanding of your gameplay loops. The basic idea is that your mechanics have to be defined around a set purpose that is flexible enough to be combined in original ways to create something not originally conceived by the developer.

Figuring out the options was just step 1 when playing *Infinifactory*. As the players unlocked new blocks by playing through the campaign, they could bring them into earlier levels to try and create new solutions. The ability to further optimize your puzzles goes back to the ranking system.

After solving a puzzle, *Infinifactory* gave players the histogram of how they compared to other players and their friends. This devious feature gave players a rough idea of where their solutions stood. The beauty of the emergent design really showed when you start looking at advanced solutions and tactics that players had discovered.

Some people created the most optimized solutions possible, while others go for devices that would make Rube Goldberg jealous. No matter what solution people came up with, so long as it satisfied the end condition, it counted as a win. Once you start going down the rabbit hole of how the game works, your understanding will forever be changed.

This is where the programming analogy fits perfectly with Zachtronics' games. Anyone who understands programming knows that as you get better at it, how you build your code will change. For the programmers reading this, it's like going from typing out all your instructions as one long command to having the program pull data into functions. Just as when it comes to writing, it can be painful to go back to your earlier work after years of refinement and growth.

The difficulty of any Zachtronics game is always focused on the players and their understanding of the mechanics. Some people will blaze right through every puzzle; others may not even get past the first stage. This is how games defined by **subjective difficulty** work, as it's up to players to make the connection themselves or hit a difficulty wall.

Just like other puzzle games, the challenges in *Infinifactory* must be conquered in the order that they're presented. Barth always orders his puzzles by an escalating complexity of design. If the player cannot figure out puzzle 3, then they won't have the understanding to then apply it to puzzle 4. Even if a player just looks up a solution, without mastering the logic behind it, she or he will become stuck again and again.

The difficulty wall was another reason why I chose Infinifactory for this listing. The other games from Zachtronics are more abstract (with the exception of *Opus Magnum*) and deal directly with programming. The issue with programming is that it can be very hard for someone who doesn't grasp programming logic to understand why something isn't working and make adjustments. As mentioned earlier, sometimes a problem in a program can come down to one variable misspelled in hundreds of lines of code. Because *Infinifactory*'s puzzles take place in a virtual space, they were a lot easier to understand and iterate on solutions.

Just as the design opened the door for creative solutions, *Infinifactory* allowed players to create their own puzzles. The game featured an editor that used the Steam Workshop to upload and download custom puzzles to the game, greatly extending its lifespan.

Emergent game design is about creating a virtual toybox of options and telling the player to go nuts. It's a concept that many developers claim to have achieved, but only a handful have actually accomplished it. To have it represented in a genre known for lacking replayability was certainly a feat. If you ever wanted to feel really smart (or stupid) while playing a game, *Infinifactory* and the rest of Zach's lineup are must-plays.

20

Doom (2016; PC and Consoles)
Fighting in Flow

The FPS genre is one of the oldest and most familiar ones to gamers. The genre drastically changed when game design became standardized over the last decade, trading in mazelike levels for linear corridors and combat. This also coincided with a push for a greater focus on storytelling. This led to the FPS genre feeling like two different titles: having a linear, single-player campaign, and then the extreme multiplayer action.

Following the just-OK *Doom 3*, the announcement of a new *Doom* for 2016 was not met with excitement. *Doom 2016* (we'll just call it *Doom* for the rest of this chapter) was both a return to form by ID Software and a lesson in designing an all-encompassing core gameplay loop.

Doom's gameplay loop has been seen many times before by previous games and its peers, but not at this level of refinement. From the very start, *Doom* presents a gameplay and main character in perfect harmony. The player is not playing as a scared civilian, or even a hardened marine; the player (male or female) is the Doom Guy: the ultimate demon-killing machine. Every weapon, power-up, and enemy kill was about making the player feel powerful.

That feeling of power was also seen in the way that *Doom* designed a silent protagonist who still had a personality. The Doom Guy just didn't care about the story, and he showed that with his mannerisms around the supporting cast. From blowing off the other characters to cocking his shotgun in one of the first cutscenes, this was a character who was not scared at all.

The personality of the Doom Guy was a big shift in tone from *Doom 3* that tried to make things more like a horror game. Many of the cutscenes in the game focused on the protagonist, with a scared look on his face. Fans of *Doom 3* most likely remember walking around slowly in the dark, with monster closets to watch out for, and of course, switching to that annoying flashlight to see. In *Doom*, the mechanics and gameplay were designed around all-out action.

Doom's core gameplay loop was a mix of old and new design. Level design was built on sprawling mazes with hidden areas, bonus objectives, and lots and lots of enemies to kill. Enemies wandered around the levels and would trap the player in a fixed area until they were killed. There was also a greater sense of verticality compared to its peers. Players would be constantly changing elevation to make their way through the levels and find secrets.

Doom was unapologetic about its arcade roots. Most shooters today have moved toward a weighted experience when it came to shooting and moving. You couldn't just run and jump and expect to hit everything perfectly, and there was a limit on the number of guns that you could have access to at any point. In turn, modern shooters have a slower pace to them compared to the high-speed era of the 1990s.

In *Doom*, the game actively encouraged the player to move at top speed, shooting enemies in every direction. So long as the weapon's crosshairs were on the enemies, chances were that the player was going to hit them. Weapons did not need to be reloaded, and the Doom Guy was free to have his entire arsenal somehow loaded and on him.

Doom focused on bringing back all the iconic enemies from previous titles, with the only exception being the summoner, who was a new character. For the enemy designs, the AI was kept basic, but that was the point; it was all about the player being aggressive and in control.

Speaking of aggression, it could be seen at its fullest in the form of the glory-kill system. FPS titles have always had trouble with balancing health as a resource and keeping the player in the fight. If the player could just regenerate at all times, then there was no challenge. However, if health was limited to fixed power-ups, it could leave the player in a weakened state for an upcoming fight. The same went for ammo, as players had to hoard ammo on their stronger guns until they were needed to fend off beefier enemies.

Doom, in an act of sheer brilliance, integrated healing recovery, ammo pickups, and killing into the glory-kill system. Finishing off enemies in specific ways would drop health or ammo to be picked up, as opposed to having to hide and recover. When any enemy had sustained enough damage, they would flash orange and be stunned for several seconds. During that time, the player could rush the enemy and perform the glory kill while being invulnerable. Early on, players got access to a chainsaw that allowed one-hit kills if they had enough fuel, with the reward being ammo for their guns.

The glory-kill system rewarded the player for being aggressive and never interrupted the flow of combat. There was never a point in *Doom* where the player should just stand still. This was a complete 180 from modern shooters, who trained players to take cover immediately when their health was low.

While most of *Doom*'s design echoed 1990s FPS games, several modern elements were added. The most modern mechanics of *Doom* would be the progression system, which rewarded players for exploring and fed directly into combat.

Each level featured multiple secrets and bonus challenges to seek. By going the extra mile, players were able to upgrade the Doom Guy in several ways. Going through the story would unlock upgrades to the player's weapons. The player had to choose between two alternative modes, each with further upgrades unlocked by using the weapon in special ways.

Bonus arenas would unlock "runes", which could be equipped to provide passive benefits like health regeneration, increased speed, and much more. Finally, players could find power cores that could be used to raise their health, ammo, and armor capacity.

There is one other important point about the progression system that we need to talk about. No matter how many times the player repeated a level, the upgrades were fixed to a single pickup. This prevented the upgrades from becoming more important than the player's skill at the game. For novices, these upgrades could help them get through a tough section, but they were not required to beat the game.

For people who wanted to see everything, the developers did an amazing job of hiding bonuses around the level. Observant players could find little Doom Dolls, and every level featured a little cutaway section from the original *Doom* series of the 1990's.

Doom was an example of the importance of figuring out, and then designing, your game around a core gameplay loop. From a design perspective, *Doom* was not a complicated game to play, but designing a game in which all the systems work harmoniously together was an example of master class design.

Doom may have been designed as one focused campaign, but its gameplay was all about two-to five-minute-long fights. The locales and the enemy groups changed, but the game was built to keep that same gameplay loop engaging from minute 1 to hour 10. *Doom* was designed to get the player into a state of absolute concentration, or the **Flow** state, for those brief periods of action.

And perhaps most important of all, *Doom* is proof that not all modern FPS games need to be built around linear experiences and design. The mazelike designs of the levels never feel confusing, thanks to the map system and the player's drive to explore. Players were always given clear direction to their next objective, but there were goodies off the beaten path.

Given the importance and utility of the secrets, it was a smart move to have upgrades that actually revealed the secrets on the map. In turn, any player, regardless of skill, could eventually find all the rewards and benefit from them.

Most surprisingly, given its pedigree and genre, even though *Doom* shipped with a multiplayer mode, the single-player campaign was praised to the extent that people preferred it to playing against their friends.

Even with this chapter, *Doom* is one of those games where the best way to understand the degree of flow is to experience it directly or indirectly. Pay attention to how the player always should be engaging the enemy and how smooth the act of shooting was. Instead of combat being a chore, *Doom* turns it into a celebration of destruction and a fully realized power fantasy.

Glossary

AAA: A designation to describe major video game studios.

Abstraction: The act of representing an event or action via in-game mechanics or systems.

Achievements: Rewards defined by the developer that players can earn for completing specific tasks while playing a game.

After action report: A narrative-focused interpretation of playing a game; typically done with the Strategy genre; abbreviated *AAR*.

AI: *Artificial Intelligence*. In Game Design, it is used to describe the behavior of enemies not controlled by another player.

ARPG: *Action role-playing game*; a title that focuses both on players actively controlling their character and character abstraction as a form of progression.

Boss rush: A type of gameplay that consists of the game only being about fighting bosses, with no other systems or mechanics.

Co-op: *Cooperative*; describes games where players are working together instead of fighting each other.

Core gameplay loop: The type of gameplay that the player will be performing the most in a game title.

Edutainment: The term combines *education* and *entertainment*; describes games that use game systems to try and teach the player a lesson.

Emergent game design: Being able to play a video game whose mechanics are flexible enough to be combined in ways not originally programmed by the developer.

Flow: Defined by psychologist Mihaly Csikszentmihalyi as a state of concentrated focus where the person loses all sense of time and space.

Free to play: A model in which a game has no upfront cost but subsists off consumers spending money on smaller in-game purchases.

Games as a Service: A model in which a game is supported through continued content developed in an attempt to keep people interested in playing it.

Gamespace: The digital environment of the game.

GDC: *Game developer's conference;* an annual event that focuses on the developers and the work that goes into game development.

Grand strategy: A style of strategy game that focuses on multiple systems of managing a large-scale operation.

JRPG: A sub-genre of role playing games that typically feature set characters and stories, along with complex game systems.

Loot table: A system designed to generate items in a video game based on a number of preset attributes; typically seen in the ARPG genre.

Mechanics: Describes the actions that the player will be performing while playing a game.

Metroidvania: A subgenre that usually combines action-based gameplay with the ability to unlock new abilities that change how the game is played over time.

Minigames: Gameplay that exists separate from the rest of a game and is used as a way to break up the normal routine of play.

Modders: People who create custom content for video games in the form of mods.

Mods: Short for modifications, any custom content created by modders for a video game.

MMO: The acronym for Massively Multiplayer Online games. A genre designed around hundreds (or thousands) of players interacting with each other.

Multisystem design: Developing a video game as a set of systems that function independent of each other, usually with some elements passing between them.

Persistence system: A game system designed to reward the player over continued plays that lead to different experiences going forward.

Procedural generation: Unique content generated by the game engine while the game is running.

PVP: *Player versus player;* describes games in which players compete with each other.

RPG: *Role-playing game;* titles of this design focus on abstraction rather than player action to determine success.

Sectional design: A philosophy of designing a game around specific sections of gameplay, as opposed to one standardized core gameplay loop.

Speed-running: Playing through a video game as quickly as possible, achieved through mastery of the game, using in-game bugs and glitches, or both.

Subjective difficulty: When the game's difficulty is based on the player's ability at it; often leads to players experiencing the same content differently.

Systems: A collection of mechanics that relate to a specific area of gameplay.

Trophy room design: An in-game representation of achievements or awards earned.

UI: *User interface;* encompasses all aspects of interacting with a video game, from the control scheme to what menus or on-screen elements are used.

Index